PLAN, RE~~SEARCH, AND~~

OUTLINE YOUR

NONFICTION BOOK IN A

DAY

Writers' Guide to Planning a Book, Researching Without Fuss, and Outlining a Nonfiction Book to Make Writing a Book Faster (Young Writers' Craft Guides Book Three)

Abraham Adekunle

Plan, Research, and Outline Your Nonfiction Book in a Day

Book and cover design by Abe A.

ISBN-13: 978-1535319584
ISBN-10: 1535319585

Second edition: July 2016

10 9 8 7 6 5 4 3 2

Contents

PART 1
INTRODUCTION

Chapter 1

Dear Reader

Dear Reader,

Thank you so much for your interest in this book.

The techniques I'm sharing with you here have helped me a lot. Maybe they'll help you some, too.

If you find a typo or two inside, please feel welcome to send me an email and let me know. I'll get right on it.

If you'd like to get my answers to any questions you may have, please feel welcome to include those, too.

My email address is in the back.

Enjoy your new book!

3

Abraham Adekunle

Best regards,
Abraham.

P.S.

I also write a weekly newsletter for young writers like myself who want to improve their craft. Please feel welcome to join us.

Chapter 2

Introduction

Admit it. You want to write your book faster. You want to write more books, make more money, and be happy. But hear this.

I failed at it when I first started writing this book. I didn't plan, didn't outline, didn't research anything, didn't...

I just jumped at the keyboard and started writing. The words were coming. In its hundreds. In its thousands. Until the thousands were five. Then the well of flow dried up. Living here in the tropics, I even thought the bright, shiny sun dried it up for me. So, I relaxed and waited for the water of flow to gather. But a day, two days, three days... nothing.

So, I sat up the fourth day and had a rethink. Something was missing. Something wasn't connecting here. I wasn't doing something right.

And what was that? **Planning, researching, and outlining.**

I know some writers outrightly detest outlining, but if you are, you'll still learn a lot from this book. You don't necessarily have to write a novel-length outline, but an outline should help you write your book faster.

Because, admit it, you want to write that book fast. You want to try a new technique. You want to write more books. And faster.

But how do you write an outline without tying yourself to list? How do you balance your pantsing with planning and outlining? Strap on your seat belt, because I'll show you.

And yes, you can do all that in a day. In fact, you can do it in a couple of hours, if you know what you're doing.

You can now write with a simple plan at hand. You can now research your book without fuss. You can now write outlines that'll help you write your book quickly.

It shouldn't be hard. It shouldn't be complicated.

Follow me as I show you how to write your book faster.

Chapter 3

Your "Why"

___

Some folks think writing a book is just for fun. Yeah, you may write for fun, but I doubt if you'll achieve something tangible with it.

You need to not only come up with ideas but know the reason for doing so. Do you want to write a book because of fame? Or ego? Or making a living? Or just as a hobby? Or you don't even know?

Furthermore, why write a kindle book at all? Are you into this because you want to mimic a popular author?

Or because someone said you can make a side income from it?

The Bitter Truth People Try to Hide

If you write because of ego, fame, or making a living, you're kidding yourself. It happens. In fact, to a lot of authors. But no guarantee. Not all writers will be famous. Not all writers will finish a book and courageously say, "I did it!" Not all writers will make a living *as a writer.*

On the flipside, if you write because you want to try making a side income on Kindle, you can. But you need a combination of content and audience to make money. You must have an offer and buyers before you can make money.

Any contradicting theory is *totally* misleading.

Now, don't decide you won't write a book just because I said that. If you want to write a book, please go ahead—the world needs more books. In fact, I'm encouraging you to do so. Why?

Let me tell you my story. Writing a paragraph without committing a hundred blunders was a fantasy. But when I took the craft seriously, my writing improved. My daily writing practice revealed the mystery of writing well. I could now use a word instead of another because, well, I could. I could now break grammar rules.

Unbelievably, it also improved my speech. I could now spot errors the way I could while writing. Sometimes, my non-native English-speaking brethren don't understand my diction. Yet, we were bred in the same country, by the same kind of teachers.

How did I separate myself from the pack? One word: **writing.** Writing made me think about writing. It made me self-conscious of what I put on the page.

But if you dwell on it alone, you may satisfy your ego, you may pride yourself to your friends, and you may be famous in your little corner—all because you've written a book. You may not just make money. You may not just be a world famous writer.

Why Should You Write a Book?

Some reasons you may want to write a book are:

1. To build credibility.
2. To build authority.
3. To gain exposure for your business.
4. To reach more people.
5. To get leads for your business.
6. To get new clients for your services.
7. To diversify your income source.

But the main reason *should be* **honing your writing skills.** Your first book will likely suck. And the second. And the third. But the more books you write, the more the latest book gets better.

Writing a book is great. In fact, you made the right decision for buying this book. After all, isn't it to help you write better and faster?

But you must also have a specific goal. If it's making money and you have your style, grammar, punctuation, and content under control, then go write that book that's been begging for life.

Just remember that you're writing simply to master your craft.

Chapter 4

The #1 Habit That Makes All the Difference

You might have already known what it is. You're here to do something specific: to change lives, to impact someone, to teach, to entertain, to educate, to demonstrate, to transport into scientific worlds.

You know you can't *not* do it. You are here **to write.**

That differentiates finishing a book or not. That differentiates acquiring customers or not. That

11

differentiates having the opportunity to make money or not.

Just thinking, discussing, or reading about writing won't make any difference.

Starting a writing session is harder than stopping (see chapter 5 for more details.) Although stopping when you're in flow also have its challenges, I'd rather choose to be able to start writing than stopping.

So, writers sigh and complain and give an excuse that if only they could start writing… Maybe that's you. Let's examine some of those excuses.

#1: I have writer's block.

Seriously? How about a 5-year-old with writer's block? I believe in writer's block, but I think you allowed it if you let it stop you for long.

Writer's block works with people's emotion. The way you feel will determine how much you write.

If you feel enthusiastic, you'll write more, better, and faster. If you feel otherwise, you'll likely write less and slower. I'm not predicting—I'm telling you what happens.

So, what caused you to write better at a time and otherwise another time? Inspiration. And you shouldn't wait for it. As I said earlier, writer's block works with your emotion. You'll discover that when you're excited and feeling as if you could toss a truck out of a highway, writer's block vanished. But once that emotion is gone, writer's block sets in.

The solution? Remove the root cause of your problem.

Is the fear of failure hindering you from writing? Pretend you don't have anything to lose. Is it the fear of mortgage? Get a job and write part time. After all, writing differentiates you from aspiring writers, not writing full time or part time.

#2: I'll start soon.

When, my friend, when? When will you conclude that research? When will you stop obsessing with planning and outlining your book?

Well, take it from someone who's been there, writing your book matters more than researching, planning, or interviewing. Because you're just curating that information for God-knows-what. If you use a percentage of it, maybe you're writing an academic paper.

What are you researching your book for? Tutorials? The content you want to give your readers? The majority of your book's content should come from your head—your mistakes, your failures, and what you've learned. Would you search Google in others' presence if you were to tell them the *exact* content of your book?

I'm not condemning researching. In fact, a part of this book deals with researching and you're fine to spend time doing it. But if it hinders you from writing, it's a barrier to your writing success.

You should start writing your book from the part you know you'll be able to handle best for now. As you write other sections or chapters, you can research along. And yes, you don't have to start writing from the introduction or first chapter.

#3: I don't have much time.

To start with, how much time do you have for writing per day? Thirty minutes? An hour? Two hours?

Some writers schedule their activities as if they're packing their luggage. Without thinking. They start with other hobbies, responsibilities, and a lot of downtimes. Then they remember that *writing's* waiting to be rescued into the luggage. But there's no more space. Or there's not enough space. So, they try to squeeze it in.

While having enough time to play and enjoy, they complain about the lack of time. Maybe that's your perfect avatar.

You need to think about your life's structure. Instead of putting writing last, put it first. You may bump it down to, say, number three if you have something **very, very** urgent demanding your attention. But it mustn't be number twenty—the luggage would've been full already.

Again, you must learn to write first. Not after checking the internet. Not after watching a video. Not after watching TV. You have to do it first. This further pushes the resistance to start your writing away as well as writer's block. You'll have more stamina to write more and longer.

For example, I noticed that after finishing housework at noon, I'm always exhausted. I would either end up sleeping in front of the computer or writing the most terrible words someone could ever read. So, I sat one day and restructured my life. Now, if I don't write in the morning before I start housework, the next session would be later in the afternoon after a nap. Since then, my body felt stronger while writing, I came with fresh enthusiasm to each writing session, and I was able to write more than before.

Other excuses writers (perhaps you!) give are:

- I don't know what to write.
- My writing isn't good enough.
- I'm too old to write.
- What if I [insert failure here].

But they're just that: excuses. You're not a writer if you keep giving excuses. At least, not yet. You become one when you sit your butt in chair and put your hands on keyboard.

You should have a valid reason for not writing. Maybe you had an accident and your two hands were bandaged, we can understand that.

But we'd know whether you're a real writer or not if your hands are scratchless, you're still healthy, and you still have your writing materials.

Chapter 5

The Friction of Starting; The Lack of Friction of Stopping

Admit it. It's part of every writer's dream.

You want to write and publish your book fast. And your next book. And the following one. So, you don't start—you *gotta* prepare, you know. You tinker around on the internet, telling yourself you're researching. You take several deep breaths like a musician at his debut concert. You put your writing materials in place, got your snacks by your side, and maybe some music.

And when you do get to writing, you pump out 10,000 words of jargon, so much that you begin to wonder how disjointed ideas could leave your fingers. What's more? You ask yourself after a seemingly endless writing session, "How do I stop? What do I say?" The words were already jargon, but you want to save yourself some embarrassment of continuing.

Because you're damn sure that someone will read those words—someone who should've become your loyal fan, who should've bought your book, and even your existing fan base. You're sure deep down that some readers will read them and abandon you forever.

Fortunately for you, I'm not immune to that also. I also feel that I should prepare fully before starting. I also want every word I write to be perfect. I also fantasize about *not needing* any round of edit.

I call that feeling the friction of starting or the lack of friction of stopping.

The friction almost grabs the tire of your writing ability and grinds it to a halt. You see the page and you immediately tell yourself that you're better off not starting right then. And when you start, summarizing the part you're writing becomes a problem.

Let's examine them.

The Friction of Starting

Have you ever ridden a bicycle? You were going very fast, and suddenly, someone magically appears on the road. You apply the brake, but the bicycle doesn't stop immediately. It screeches a few meters ahead before burying the front tire into the earth.

That's the perfect picture of friction in work. It stops something, but almost immediately.

Every time you apply the brake of excuse, your writing bicycle doesn't stop right away, but does **almost immediately, in the twinkling of an eye.** Or to be precise, it will bury its front tire in a mess. And to get back on your writing feet, you'll have to pedal—get back in flow.

So, how exactly can you stop this friction? It's simple, even ridiculous. Stop applying the brake when in writing mode.

Brakes can sometimes be research or not finding time to write, or any of the excuses writers give not to write.

Identify the brakes you're involuntarily applying to your writing bicycle. If you find that you research too much, that's the brake, simply turn off the Wi-Fi, remove the broadband internet modem, or anything you use to connect to the internet.

You might think it's a silly advice, but that's the only advice I can give you about this issue. Some writers may get so fanatic about it that they tell you to "just put your butt in chair and hands on keyboard." It's not a bad advice, but it doesn't address what it should.

How do you exactly remove the internet modem you're using when you've tried so many times without success? That's the issue of your willpower. But we're not talking about willpower here. We're strictly talking about what causes you not to start writing sooner, and how to stop it.

If you feel like you have willpower problem (that is, you can't resist almost every temptation that comes your way), then every aspect of your life will also suffer because of it. If you discover that you have a problem, please, go get help from someone, perhaps a doctor or therapist. Aside that, you're good to go on this.

Before I began to write this chapter, I had my internet on and I was reading an advice from someone who's made it in the self-publishing industry. She's written a number of stories, she continues to write every day, and she's amassed a host of readers. What was I doing reading a popular writer's memoir when I'm still at book three?

I took a deep breath and yanked off the poor internet modem from my laptop. Now I've written over 600 words. If I hadn't yanked off the modem, I know I wouldn't have written a word.

Identify the brake. Stop applying it. Will it work all the time? Not at first. But after some time, it would become a regular habit.

The Lack of Friction of Stopping

Unlike applying a brake to your bicycle, lack of friction is just like pedaling on a freeway, going almost 100 miles an hour (oh, my!) Before you know it, you sighted where you're going, but when you apply the brake, it doesn't stop right away; it doesn't even stop a few meters ahead. Why? Because you've accelerated much more than when you started.

Have you heard about inertia? It means struggling to start and struggling to stop. I thought starting was all it takes, that you would know when to stop, that everything will take care of itself when you start punching keys.

But no. Inertia kicks in. Maybe you've been going about 2 miles an hour when you started, the power of inertia will make the experience very pleasurable that all you could do is accelerate more and more. (That's one of the popular causes of accidents: speed. Speed may also kill your endings in writing.)

So, you wait till the bicycle decelerate. In other words, you have to you're your destination and still speed some meters ahead before stopping.

In writing, that means more rant, more ramble, more unwanted words. And you can't help it.

Well, let's see how to tackle that.

Do you know how to structure a section of whatever you write? It's below:

- Tell 'em what you're going to tell 'em.
- Tell 'em.
- Tell 'em what you told 'em.

Simple, but not easy. First, you tell your readers what you're going to tell them, just the way I've told you that we'll be talking about the friction of starting and the lack of friction of stopping in this chapter.

That could be starting with an attention-grabbing statement or quote. That could be asking a thought-provoking question. That could be making a bold claim, making people label you a troublemaker. But it all boils down to one thing: identifying the problem.

Because, let's face it, if you aren't solving any problem in your nonfiction book, then what's the point? You're strictly writing to solve your readers' problem, to ease a bit of their life.

What you do next doesn't matter, provided you solve the problem. In other words, provided you tell 'em. It doesn't matter if you agitate the problem, as copywriting gurus do. It doesn't matter if you warm 'em of not asking or not reading what you're going to tell 'em. What matters is that you tell 'em.

And when you're done telling them, tell 'em what you told 'em. Just as I'll tell you what I've already told you here.

You might think, "Oh, that's a serious business of repetition!" Yes, it is, but what isn't repetition nowadays? Writing about starting and tying a piece of writing together doesn't mean someone hasn't written about it before. But it will remind those who's read some other materials about it, and inform others. Likewise, the brain needs repetition to take note of the key points.

You see, if you don't structure your writings that way, your readers, who actually read it word-for-word, may forget what they've just read by the time they're done. So, what do you do?

Simple: you tell them what you've told them. This may be having another subhead, "Summary" or "Conclusion." This might be a couple of paragraphs serving the same purpose. Just tell 'em what you told 'em.

Summary

The friction of starting to write is just like riding a bicycle and applying the brake while pedaling; the bicycle will stall. So, to stop the friction, you identify the brake (which is usually an excuse, like not finding the time to write) and you try all your best to stop applying the brake. It will compel you to pedal without stalling.

The lack of friction of stopping is just like riding a bicycle on a freeway, pedaling away at an enormous 100 meters an hour (although, that's gross); you won't be able to stop at your destination when you want to.

Instead, you'll have to go farther, which in your writing means more unnecessary words.

Fortunately, the workaround is to have the end in mind. You simply rehearse what you've told your readers some minutes ago and you'll be done with that section.

Note: The standard format of a piece of writing was adapted for easy understanding. Look, for example:

- Introduction.
- Body.
- Conclusion.

And look at this:

- Tell 'em what you want to tell 'em.
- Tell 'em.
- Tell 'em what you told 'em.

Which is more understandable?

PART 2

PRE-PLANNING STAGE

CHAPTER 6

The #2 Elements of a Bestselling Idea

I always thought finding the perfect idea, or buying a software (although, that could help) makes a bestselling idea.

There's no bestselling idea. It may be a bestselling one, I agree, but you have to do your part like writing a good book, setting up your launch team, promoting it like hell, etc. to make it to the list. So, no idea is bestselling of itself; you make it a bestselling one by your effort.

That said, how could we, authors who don't have the luxury of spending thousands of dollars on promoting our books, find an idea that'll sell well.

First, where do ideas come from?

This differs with every writer. I may get ideas while taking a walk. You may get yours by surfing around on forums. But knowing where ideas come from is a ridiculous question.

The question is, "how do you confirm that the ideas you conceive will sell?" There are only two ways to know:

- Buzz.
- Content.

Before you throw pillows my way, see the explanation below.

Let's say I love beadmaking, and I want to write a book about it. First, we'll check the internet, which is the medium you'll be using to sell that book, for people interested in that topic.

A fast way is to check the sales rank of related books on Amazon and check how many books there are on that topic.

You could check to confirm an idea will sell on:

- Amazon.
- Quora.
- Yahoo Answers.
- YouTube.
- Kobo, Nook, iBook, etc.

- Forums on beadmaking, if there are any. (Search for "forum:beadmaking" without quotes on Google.)
- Blogs on beadmaking, if there are any. (Search for "blog:beadmaking" without quotes on Google.)

One of these two things would have happened after checking all those platforms:

- The idea won't sell.
- Several books on the topic are selling.

First, if you confirm that the idea will sell, that means there'll be some other books to study, both content and reviews. Second, that means books on that topic are selling well.

If you find that, for example, a book on the topic you want to write has a sales rank below #20,000 on Amazon, you should look into it.

(Just a note: I checked Amazon and couldn't find a beadmaking book selling well. Stunning, only 35 search results in all of Yahoo Answers database, a clear warning to run for your dear life.)

But here's another problem. "There's no sign that the ideas I keep conceiving will sell," you say. "There's no book on the topic and no content on forums like Quora."

Well, let me tell you the secret to maintaining a fair balance between what's selling and what you're passionate about.

Find Your Area of Inpertise

Here's an excerpt from my book, *Generate and Validate Your Bestselling Idea:*

> Lest I forget, I checked my dictionary, but I couldn't find the word "Inpert."
>
> The word originated when I was brainstorming with my mentor. The idea was that since you're not an "expert" yet, you can be an "inpert." Which means that instead of wearing the same wig with a college professor, you can come off as reporting what ordeal you went through, how you learned what you're narrating now, what worked for you, and what did not.
>
> Simply put, an **inpert** is:
>
> Someone who doesn't appear as a Know-It-All, but who, with a conscious state of mind, commits to learning every day and helping others learn what he's also learned.
>
> Your area of inpertise can be anything. Remember that you're learning and the tribe following you is learning as you.
>
> Have you been studying how to write a Kindle book lately, but you don't yet have a slew of Kindle books under your belt? You can relate your experience.
>
> Tell us why your techniques didn't work, if it didn't. Tell us why it worked, if it did. Tell us the "smart cuts" you'd have taken to learn it faster. This itself opens doors to whatever you've been learning, whether a hobby or not, and that you're passionate about.

So, you can look at topics that are selling out there
and pick a topic that you're interested in and try doing it
yourself, and then narrate what you learned, what
worked, and what didn't work for you.

Summary

So, the two essential elements in an idea are,
interested readers and other contents created on that
same topic.

You can check eBook publishing platforms and see
what books are selling, and balance that with what
you're passionate about. That is, finding your area of
"inpertise."

Chapter 7

How to Create an Irresistible Title

An irresistible title is inevitable in a successful book. It has to call out to potential readers, just along with the book cover. The title is the first feature of a book that readers notice. Even when they notice the cover first, they look at it for the book's title.

So, you'll want your book title to spell out what your book is about.

The Purpose of an Irresistible Title

A compelling book title does two things:

- It makes browsers click. Browsers on eBook retailing sites are looking for a specific thing—a solution. If the title doesn't tell them, "I can solve your problem," they won't give it a chance. The title goes hand-in-hand with a beautiful cover.

  Does a book have an amateurish cover? Readers may click. An awkward title? It may repel readers away from your book.

- It makes the book discoverable in search results. If you go over to the Amazon search bar and type in a keyword like "outline" and you put a space after the word, a drop-down list would appear with suggestions, which is what readers are using to look for a solution.

  Take this book, for example. The specific keyword for this type of book is "outline a nonfiction book." If you want to make your book discoverable, you have to incorporate the keyword into the title. Hence, the title of this book: *Plan, Research, and **Outline Your Nonfiction Book** in a Day*. If someone searches for that keyword, there's much chance that it will show up than a book with the title, "*Learn How Outlining Can Help You*

Write a Book Faster." If someone types the phrase, "outline a nonfiction book," the book may likely show up on page 2 and beyond in search results.

So, what factors should you consider when you want to create a title for your book?

1. Make a Big Promise

In Chapter 11, I talked about what to research for your book, among whom is giving your readers an avatar. One of the questions deals with what urgent problem your readers have and what outcome you want to give them after reading your book.

So, write the urgent problem your readers are encountering on a notepad (or anywhere you scribble.) Beside it, write the outcome your readers would have after reading your book. For example:

Urgent problem: want to write a book fast.
Outcome: plan, research, and outline that book in just a day. No wasting of time.

Please, and please, do not make a promise your book cannot fulfill. Otherwise, bad and negative reviews may nip it in the bud, and it won't help you in the long run.

2. Use a Benefit-Driven Title

What benefit is your book offering to your readers? You have to distinguish between benefit and features. A

feature is *"this book contains a step-by-step guide on outlining a book."* A benefit is *"this book will help you outline a book from a vague idea in a day."*
Examples of benefit-driven titles are:

- ***How to Write a Book From Start to Finish Line***. This title quickly sells you on the fact that it will help you outline your book *from start to finish*. Who doesn't love getting things done? The author knows that people want to finish writing their book. They want to publish it, hold it in their hands, and say, "I did this." And it all starts with finishing the book outline.

- **How to Start a Successful Blog in One Hour.** This title capitalizes on the benefit: "starting a successful blog" and it gives the reader a specific time to achieve that: "one hour." Starting a blog doesn't mean success, but it matters a lot. If you get it right, you'll be heading the right way.

- **How to Write a Nonfiction eBook in 21 Days - That Readers LOVE!** This title makes what seems to be a daunting task, "writing a book," easier, even promising a finished book in 21 days. Readers get that benefit from it. If they actually write a book in 21 days, they'll hold it in their hands, and shout, "I did it!" on rooftops.

- **How to Sell Using The Six Power Sellers.** Was there something called "the six power sellers"? I bet you didn't know. Me neither.

So, this title clearly states that the book has a
secret called "the six power sellers." And what
is the benefit you'll get from it? You'll achieve
what seems impossible: "sell."

3. Make it Flow

This is how your title sounds to your readers. You'll
want to use a short, memorable title, because:

- It's easy to remember.
- It's short and to the point.
- It fits your book cover well.

Imagine how this title would sound: ***"How to Plan
Your Nonfiction Book after Getting an Idea,
Research The Hell Out of It Even If You Don't Know
Nada About It, And Outline Everything In Order to
Write Fast."***
Compare it to this title: **"Plan, Research, and
Outline Your Nonfiction Book in a Day."**
First, the former title is harder to pronounce, while
the latter sounds better. Even the first four words in the
title say it all. Second, the latter title would fit the cover
very well, while the latter would have the hardest time
accommodating the author name.
Look at how this titles below flow:

- ***Think and Grow Rich***
- ***The 4-Hour Workweek***
- ***The $100 Startup***
- ***The Art of War***
- ***The Art of Work***

- *Headline Hacks*

4. Arouse Their Curiosity

To achieve this, make a big claim. For example, "Be 10% More Happier in 24 Hours." What? How can this book tell me I can be 10% happier in 24 hours?

You should only do this if you can deliver on your promise. Otherwise, you're signaling to bad reviews.

See examples of titles that arouse curiosity below:

- *I Hope They Serve Beer in Hell.* What? With all we've been told about Hell? With all the horrors described of Hell, this author still wants to go there. In fact, he wants to know if his favorite drink is available over there. (Fact check, this is a fiction book title, but it can well work with nonfiction, too.) There's something in you that wants to find out what he meant by that statement.

- *Why Men Love bitches.* Oh, there we go again. Why would a sensible man like me love a bitch? A male reader would likely ask himself that question after seeing that title. Would it apply to me? Have I loved bitches in the past? Am I currently loving bitches? What are the reasons?

5. Incorporate Specific Keywords in the Title

Last, but not the least, your title must contain a specific keyword because readers will discover your book that way. For example, below are titles with the keywords bolded in them:

- *My **Blog Traffic** Sucks!* by Steve Scott

- *How to **Outline Your Book** From Start to Finish*

- *How to **Lose Weight** Fast in 10 Simple Steps*

- ***Make Money Writing** Kindle Books*

What Your Subtitle Should Contain

A book's subtitle is not required to be on the book cover, so it can contain as many keywords as possible. Even if you hadn't use any keyword in the main title, the subtitle is a freer space to blow your book's horn.
To do this, ask yourself these questions:

- What is the urgent problem I'm solving for my readers right now?

- What is the outcome they will have after reading and following what's in my book?

When you know the answers to the questions above, you'll be able to elaborate more on what your book is about and what it will do more for your readers. Below are examples of subtitles elaborating more on what the book will do for its readers:

- *My Blog Traffic Sucks!* **8 Simple Steps to get 100,000 Visitors without Working 8 Days a Week**

- *The 4-Hour Workweek:* **Escape 9-5, Live Anywhere, And Join The New Rich**

- *The $100 Startup:* **Reinvent the Way You Make a Living, Do What You Love, and Create a New Future**

Action Steps

- Brainstorm ten or more titles. You don't have to do this when you're tired or while writing. You may end up changing a seemingly perfect title while a seemingly terrible one might be the best for you. Rest before you do this because you do need your brain performing at its best.

- Test for flow. Pronounce the title of your book. You'll know which sounds awkward. Can you rework the title? Can you change some words?

- Do the book cover test. I recommend that you go over to MS Word and resize the page to fit the size of your book cover and write out the keywords on the page. How big can it get before it's truncated? How wide does it go? Can you see the title while in thumbnail size?

- Ask your audience. If you already have readers or email subscribers, you can create a survey, describe the book, and tell them you're seeking a preference between titles.

- Go with your heart. Having completed all the steps above, you might feel tempted to agonize over the title, but the truth is that you can always change the title and subtitle in the future.

PART 3
PLANNING YOUR BOOK

Chapter 8

Introduction to Planning Your Book

What is planning?

Planning means a lot more than outlining a book, which first comes to writers' minds. Talk about organizing a folder on your hard drive, binding your physical documents together, and the like, it's part of planning your book.

Imagine traveling from Shrek's swampy Drury Lane to the kingdom of Far Far Away. And imagine that you didn't know the route, nor had a map, nor scheduled what you would be doing.

You can't just rush onto the way. You have to plan, which the first tasks would be getting a map. Then you'd plot your way. And then you pack your luggage and leave. Now see what the items on the plan list would look like:

Plan, Research, and Outline Your Nonfiction Book in a Day

- Find the best map in the land.
- Plot my way to Far Far Away.
- Pack necessary things I'd need on the way.
- Begin traveling.

Now that seems simplistic. But it's never an outline. An outline is an order you'd travel. For example, the outline from Drury Lane to Far Far Away could be:

- The Forest of Dragons.
- Bridge over the burning lava.
- The village of the magicians.
- A bit of forest.
- Far Far Away.

Did you see the difference between an outline and a plan? The plan clearly lists what you'd do to boost your chance of surviving on the journey while the outline lists the order in which you'd travel through the map.

If you check your dictionary, you'll see that plan means preparing or a decision to do something. According to the Longman Dictionary of Contemporary English, the word "plan" means:

> *INTENTION: something you have decided to do.*

Likewise, you also have to plan—to decide—to make your book work.

Imagine you want to write a weight loss book. You can't just decide what your book will contain. Chances are, you'll even tweak what you think is the best outline you've written, no matter how hard you try to stick to it.

So, you can't guarantee that you'd end up following that outline, after all.

In other words, you may plot your way from Drury Lane to Far Far Away but may fail to follow it due to inevitable factors. Fortunately, that's good news for you. Why? Because you don't always have to draw an outline upfront. Not that you wouldn't. You'll just have a rough outline.

When you think of outline, I'm sure you're thinking of the Table-of-Contents section of your book. You can't have that until you finish your book.

What isn't planning?

Many writers still confuse the meaning of an important writing process: planning a book.

It isn't outlining, the way some think. Why? Because planning is what you do first before writing an outline for your book. The process goes thus:

Find ideas >> Confirm that it will sell >> Plan it >> Reseach it >> Draw a first draft outline

You may think you can closely follow up your outline if you do it first, but I disagree. Something as simple as a research may nullify your outline. You may have to move things around, add some chapters, or omit some sections that don't belong in the book.

Again, researching isn't planning, because you're working to unveil an outline. Simply put, research is and should be part of your plan. Take the plan that'll get you from Drury Lane to Far Far Away, for example. You'll have to search for the best map in the land. That's an equivalent of researching.

Most of all, planning isn't organizing your files and documents, it's part of it. Imagine only packing luggage prior to the journey to Far Far Away. That's part of it. It's even necessary. But not until the third item.

Packing luggage is the equivalent, for example, of testing which writing software is good for you. Is it MS Word? Or Scrivener? Or yWriter5? That's just finding and organizing what you think you'll use on the journey (writing), but you still have to find a map (which is the equivalent of researching what's out there.)

On the flipside, here's what planning is (but not entirely is):

- Setting deadlines.
- Organizing your files.
- Sketching your idea.
- Indicating what you'll need to research for the book.
- Drawing a rough outline.
- …and so on.

Note that working your plan is different from planning. If I organize my files, research, and create a rough outline, I'm working my plan.

When Do I Plan My Book?

The word "plan" itself suggest preparation for something coming up in the future. Obviously, it's after you validate your idea.

You're more likely to abandon your book if you ignore planning your book and working your plan. In fact, many authors began planning their book months before sketching their idea.

For example, they build launch teams and create awareness for their book.

Why I don't believe in pantsing.

I read on Jim butcher's LiveJournal(http://jimbutcher.livejournal.com/2880.html) about the brain reflex's psychology. It reacts thus:

Reaction >> Reason >> Anticipation >> Choice

So let's say an idea struck me (mind you, a pantser) from the blue. My first reflex would be **"Reaction"** which could be: "Wow! A kindle book about losing weight? Woohoo!"

And my brain would give me the **"Reason"** it's super-, duper-awesome: "Who would have thought I could lose fifty pounds in a week? I can write this."

Then it would signal an **"Anticipation"** and I could think, "Hey, what am I waiting for? Let me start telling this fatties how I lost weight and how they can lose theirs, too."

Then as a pantser, I'd decide that I *cannot not* wait to write the book, because well, the next thing a pantser do is put butt in chair and start writing. No plan, no outline, no nada, nothing.

Here's the shocker: **my brain just planned the process for me.**

Thinking about my weight-loss experience is just a guise for thinking of the looming book's content. Because I'd lost weight recently, my brain suggested it as the content. If I have no experience like that, my brain would suggest another. "How about researching?" my brain could say.

What I've done is turn my brain into a planning machine. And even if I tinker around on the internet, Googling about what I wanted to write about, the truth is that I've just followed the process laid out in this book:

- Plan (with the help of my brain.)
- Research.
- Store the outline also in my brain (or maybe I have an unorganized rough idea map.)

All because of pantsing.

Oftentimes, we "pantse" because we're tired of the hard work and because our brain has kicked into overdrive mode. You could pump out 5,000 words at that moment, but it could also haunt you for the next three weeks.

Let me tell you something about me. The first book I wanted to write was titled, "Setting The Words." That was back in 2014 when I first delved into the world of writing. Because I was a novice, and because I was quite lazy to plan, I did what was supposed to come last, maybe even after writing the first draft. I wrote a final outline. And I tried all my best to stick with it, but I couldn't finish it. What a big mistake.

Personally, I believe we're all planners and outliners, but just have our balance. People who report they do well pantsing may have a retentive memory, second to none—even to an android.

If you believe you're not an outliner or a planner, then you're entitled to your belief. I don't outline aggressively. In fact, the outline I drew for this book

51

changes as I write it. But you're reading this book, right? How could that be possible?

I planned. I spent a good number of days planning and researching this book before I begin to write. I write at my normal speed and I'm sure I'll wake up tomorrow to continue it. If you're reading this book, it means my planning paid off.

Ignore thinking that you're not a planner, because you may not even need an outline until you finish writing your book. But you need to plan for it, like FIFA plan for every Football World Cup.

Plan first, preferably before you outline. You could meditate for a couple of days. But you must plan. First.

Chapter 9

How to Plan Your Book

What Should I Plan in or for My Book?

This is a million dollar question. I can't possibly stand behind this pulpit of a book, look down on you, and say, "Thou shalt plan **this** for your book and **that** in your book."

Most times, your creative instinct will tell you what you need to plan. You should follow your instinct, if so. You may find that you're not just good in organizing your documents, but you still know where what is. You could plan some things, even if you're not a planner.

I didn't plan how I'd research this book, but I researched a little to help me start writing (cue friction of starting.) This book's research is complicated. Every time I notice something in a book or article, I'd think I have to write something about it. So, I'll be researching as I write, as well as deciding what goes in the book or not.

If I had outlined, I would've shot myself in the foot.

Now the problem will be battling myself back to the keyboard while researching. If you know you can't stand brisker research temptations, then do it first.

Again, you may need to research while writing, especially if the content relies more on research. Well, I'd say you should choose what suits you. If you decide only to research before you start writing, you may need it much. If you decide to research as you write, the problem is getting back to the keyboard.

Weigh both. Choose what suits you.

How to Plan Your Book

1. Organize Your Files

You have to organize your files and documents, whether you use a virtual or physical document. Just as a house has apartments and rooms in the right place, your files should also be organized for easy navigation.

For instance, let's say you're using a virtual document—files on your hard drive—you'll need to:

- Create one folder with the name of your book. You shouldn't force yourself to create a final title at this stage because you're just starting.

For this book, the working title I'm using is, "Plan, Research, and Outline."

Although, I may not end up using it as the final title, it helps me organize my book files. Whenever I want to do anything related to the book, I know where to go—the folder.

I recommend you put the folder where you can easily find it. I tend to forget things like that, so I had to create nested layers of folders like **My Books >> Plan, Research, and Outline >> Cover**. And it works for me. If you prefer to use this method, you'll need this later on when you're writing, editing, proofreading, and even publishing your book.

I realized its importance when I tried to use free promotion sites to promote one of my Kindle books. You'll be uploading covers, copying and pasting book descriptions, and supplying ASINs. If you have an easily accessible folder, it won't pose any problem to you.

- Create folders in the mother folder with appropriate labels.

While dealing with your book, you'll have to do different things other than writing the book itself. You'll have to create folders for covers, print version, etc.

It's useful if, like me, you're a DIY author—
you do everything yourself.

Take designing a book cover, for example.
While designing the cover, I save different
versions of the cover I like. And when I'm
done, I have to convert it into a picture format.
Many times, I've ended up stuffing the mother
folder with cover files.

So, I create another folder inside the parent
directory with the label "Cover," so every
cover I design goes inside it. Even inside the
cover folder, I have some other folders with
labels like "Former" and "Print."

The bottom line here is to do what works for
you. That works for me, so I do it. Do what
works for you so that we both end up
organizing our book files.

If you're using a physical document, it's a no-brainer
that you should have a binder to keep all your scribbles
together. Also, consider labeling your documents in the
header area, so that if mixed with other documents,
you'll quickly recognize it.

I use both physical and virtual folders, but I'm still
trying my best to adhere to the organizing rule as
regarding physical document (well, it's not a rule
because it's not required. But it makes writing your book
easier.)

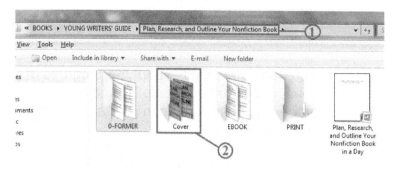

2. Organize a Launch Team

Don't let the thought of organizing a launch team intimidate you. Do you have a platform of loyal fans? Platforms like your email list, blog, social media followers? Then you should build a team that would help you spread the word.

Here are benefits of having a launch team:

- Build awareness for your book, even before you've written a word.
- Build a waiting list of customers.
- Launch your book with lots of reviews.
- Leverage word-of-mouth advertising.
- Curating beta readers.

There's no better feeling than having your fans pay for a book before you've written a word. Here are some of the ways you can organize your team:

- Have a separate email list for them. With the push of a button, you can email your fans and just segment them into another list based on an action like clicking a button. So why shouldn't you?

You can send emails about the progress of your book, what you're up to, and how the process is going. You can give a pep talk to your team.

- Let them know they're on the list, why they're on it, and what they'll be receiving. Clarity rules in all forms of communication. Ignore your subscribers and a bunch of them will unsubscribe. Simply tell them the reason they're on another list and talk only about your book to that segment of your fans. You should also have a note at the end of your emails to them stating that they're receiving that email because they decided to be part of your launch team.

3. Plan Your Time

As I said earlier, when someone mentions the phrase "planning your book," many writers think it's "outlining your book." It's evident in the Google searches I did. No related search at the end of the page has "plan" as a keyword, as at this time of writing. Instead, Google replaced "planning" with "outlining."

It also showed in the articles I read. Most articles prioritized outlining a book. The whole phenomenon could change your belief. But I still disagree with anyone equating outlining with planning a book. Sure, it's part of the process, but not entirely the process.

Plan, Research, and Outline Your Nonfiction Book in a Day

You should consider planning your time as you plan other aspects of your book. Otherwise, you'll just be working without recording your progress or the amount of time it took you to write different books.

Some writers already plan their time. Some still wrangle with it. But aggressive timeplanning won't work for everybody. You should plan your time because:

- It will help you determine what is wasting your time. Maybe you research to the extreme, or you tinker around on the internet without a purpose, your timeplan will tell you where it's happening.

- It tells what you should be doing when. When you plan your time, you'll not only know when you should be writing, but you'll know other writing-related things you should be doing, like doing more research, editing, etc.

- It gives you your goal in bitesize chunks. You may plan to write 2,000 words everyday for five days to write a book of approximately 8,000 words. Suddenly, you won't be seeing the 10,000 words before you anymore. You'll be seeing 2,000 words instead. If you plan each day, say, into four sessions, again, you won't see 2,000 words anymore. You'll be seeing 500 words, which you should be able to finish in 45 minutes at most.

  Now let's say you write first at dawn, after breakfast, after lunch, and before you sleep, your typical writing day will be easy to you.

You wake up and you bang out five hundred words. At 10 AM, you bang out another. At 3 PM, you do the same thing. And at 8PM, you do the same thing. That's easy, if you ask me.

That's the power of planning aforehand. You not only know your writing sessions, but you give time for other things that needed to be in place before writing. Maybe you have to research as you write, read before you write, or want to have a nice time. You'll be able to do all that when you plan your time.

Now imagine what the process would be like if you plan to finish the same book in two weeks.

Your session will be reduced to twice a day. Or even once, where you'd write a thousand word straight. You can even have weekends off. Because you'd have planned it.

Now imagine you were to just ruminate on an idea in your brain, draw up a one-line-per-idea outline, and start punching the keyboard. You won't know the amount of research you need, because, let's face it, you can't write a book without researching, no matter how small. You won't know what you have to cover and what doesn't relate to your book at that moment.

That alone may nosedive everything. You
may find that you need a lot of research and
that researching that topic would take time
and more effort. Or you may go researching
never to return to the keyboard.

You may discover that what you're writing
doesn't appeal to anyone, after all. (Cue
writer's block!)

You lose everything you've invested in that
book if that happens.

- Planning your time builds your momentum.
  Do you know that there's more chance that
  you'll finish your book if you look at your
  progressing progress every day?

  What I mean is, imagine you want to write a
  10,000-word book in five days. Day 1, you log
  two thousand words. Day 2, you do the same.
  Same with Day 3. By Day 3, your brain won't
  be looking at the 2,000 words you're logging
  anymore. It would be analyzing the total word
  count, which would be 6,000, and worrying
  over the remaining, which would be 4,000.

  Your brain would tell you, "Hey, you wrote
  6,000 words in three days. It's just two days
  to go!" From then on, you'd be looking at
  nothing but the finish line, which would be
  10,000 words.

As you've seen, you should plan your time, even when you're not writing a book. Here's how you can plan your time:

- Set a deadline. If you don't set it and work toward it, you won't know whether you can achieve it or not. In fact, if you don't set deadlines on anything, you'll be working as if you have all the time in the world, which you (partially) don't have.

  Your book needs to be out in the world, not too early, and neither too late. You want to balance your starting time and finish time so that you have the freedom to polish your manuscript.

  Ever wonder why so many books have typography errors in them? Because their authors didn't set reliable deadlines. It could be either too early or too late. But authors are likely to set an early deadline, maybe because of the fresh enthusiasm of starting their book.

  In that case, authors would rush through their book because they want to publish it on time. When authors set late deadlines, they may likely slack in working toward it, because, you know, there's still time. And when they see the day approaching, they rush through the process or, worse, abandon the book.

But *"worstest"* is not setting a deadline at all. The two kinds of deadlines mentioned are still better, though not preferable. An author could still publish their books whether they set deadlines or not. But if you don't set deadlines at all, you may not finish any project, whether that's finishing your resume or cleaning your house.

I don't recommend rushing through a book, but it's just better than not finishing and publishing your book.

Take this book, for example, I started writing it (mind you, writing; not planning) on April 6th 2016 and I set a deadline to finish the first draft in two weeks. Now let's say this book were to be a 20,000-word book. That equals writing approximately 1,500 words in a day.

Let me tell you something. I wrote about 2,000 words on the first day, which is yesterday as at this time of writing. Will there be days I won't achieve 1,500 words a day? Absolutely. But, wait let me check the word count…

It's now about 4,000 words. That means I've already written ahead of my daily goal by more than 60%. Are you starting to see how my brain is analyzing the word count thing? It's not seeing 4,000 words. It's seeing the remaining 16,000 words.

Overall, I'm likely to finish the first draft in two weeks. I may finish before the deadline or a little after the deadline, but finishing the first draft is what matters. I'm sure you'll know that after finishing this draft, I'll be setting another deadline for editing, proofreading, designing the cover, writing the book description, etc.

By then, I would draw another timeplan when I won't be writing any first draft, which I think could span a week.

- Schedule writing sessions. You may not want to do this but it can help you a lot. I don't schedule my individual writing sessions. I just focus on writing everyday.

  There are days you won't want to write. Scheduling your sessions could rescue you. If you do it, you'll just have to adhere to the schedule. (Don't be late to the appointment, okay?)

  Joanna Penn uses a physical diary to plan her time. And some other authors are likely using that method, too. If you know it will work for you, do it. If you know it won't work for you…

- Set a daily word count. This may resemble scheduling writing sessions, but it's not, and in a unique way.

In scheduling, you plan your writing sessions, whether twice or a hundred times. But in a daily word count, you do nothing than focus on meeting your daily goal. You could set a daily word count by dividing the total word count of your manuscript by the total number of days you want to dedicate to writing the book. Of course, you won't know the exact word count you'll publish your book, but you can provide an estimate based on your instinct, previous works, and feats you want to attain.

So, for my own book, the daily word count could be:

$$20,000/14 = 1,429$$

That's approximately 1,500 words, so that's what I'll be focusing on every single day.

How to Make Planning Your Time Work: Factors to Consider

If you loathe planning especially a flexible commodity like time, then you may not want to follow the idea of planning your time. But to be able to finish your book, you must work on it consistently. Day after day.

Could you miss a day of writing? Of course. Could you miss two days in a row? Well, if you can make up for it either by working three times faster or by postponing your deadline. But if you will still accomplish something—finishing your book—you have to work on it consistently.

I've talked about how your brain calculates the remaining time to the finish line. Before your brain does that, you'll have to battle through the launch, just like a rocket. The takeoff may seem hard and the rocket has to battle gravity and inertia.

But when it rises higher and higher, gravity diminishes. Instead, the opposing force now aids it.

Writing your book works that way. Initially, it would be hard to write, but as you write more and more, the resistance to write that book diminishes, especially if you're writing a short book.

Take, for example, I'm over 6,000 words into this book and I'm aiming at 20,000. Has the resistance to write diminished?

Short answer: no.

Medium answer: no, but it's just as if it isn't there.

Long answer: no. The resistance I have to battle now is starting individual writing sessions. Once I got past that, I don't feel any more force working against me. I see 6,000 words and my brain tells me, "Hey, you're 14,000 words to go." And as I write more and more, the resistance continues to diminish.

Granted, I don't check word counts every time, but once I caught sight of it, it lifts my spirit. I think, "If I can get that done, I can write the remaining words. I'm closer to the finish line." Unlike the Law of Diminishing Return.

But why did I experience something like that? Because I work consistently. If I miss a day of writing, you bet that inertia will creep up my arms.

"Hey," you say, "I don't have enough time."

What? Let's tackle that first.

Short Writing Sessions Still Matter

If you're so busy that all you can spare in a day is 30 minutes, should you still go ahead?

Yes, but if…

- You know what you want to write.
- You have privacy during that time.
- You can focus.

First, can you write something meaningful in 30 minutes? Yeah, but you could end up cutting it if you don't plan aforehand. That's why planning your book is important. Putting your button chair with your writing materials in front of you is productive, but knowing what to write right then is more productive.

So, I advise you to plan your book before you begin writing if you can't spare much time. Even if a simple chapter outline and a sentence to accompany each chapter is all you can do, it's still better.

Second, you should have necessary privacy. Some writers claim that they can write in spite of distractions. Um, really? They say they can write in front of TV, in the presence of family members, with their phone nearby.

I hear. If the TV doesn't disturb my writing, they say, it's not a distraction. If I can answer my kids without stopping my typing, they say, then they're not a distraction. If I can hang the phone between a shoulder and an ear and still type, they say, it's not a distraction.

But how many writers are immune to that. TV, kids, phone, neighbors, the internet, all that. You'll probably adopt the commandments of the monks to be immune to every distraction, but you can do it an easier way.

You could set up a private writing environment.
As I write this, three of my siblings are in the sitting
room, running around, each step making a thumping
sound like an elephant's. But does it affect me? You bet
not. They're doing their thing and I'm doing mine. Win-
win. If they knock on the door and I don't answer, they
know that I'm busy right away.

I urge you to try that for yourself. Plan what you want
to write and get some privacy.

Third, focus. So you've just come back from work—
hectic day, angry boss, irritating coworkers, endless
traffic. Arggh!

If you come to your writing desk like that, you won't
write effectively. What's the point in writing what you will
cut later?

If you know your days are like that, and that you
can't spare more than 30 minutes, 45 at most, can you
change your writing time? I'm so productive in the
evenings. Talk about anything from 4 PM to midnight,
even to the wee hours of the morning, I'm game, and
coffee supports me. You may not be like that. You may
be a morning person, as they say. Can you wake up 30
minutes early? Forty-five minutes early? What about an
hour?

The trick is to wake up to write before commencing
your normal day. That way, you won't have to worry
about writing in the evening after a hectic day at work.

Be Willing to Adapt

I said "adapt" because "change," is another thing.
For example, your schedule may change, you may be
traveling when you have to write, or you may have an

emergency. Don't let that stop you. Rework your
timeplan, but watch out for something…

…**not writing consistently.**

Whatever hindering you from writing daily and
boosting your enthusiasm is an enemy to your project.

Sure, you can choose between your writing and that
urgent calling. Still, whatever happens, writers write. No
matter what happens.

Terrorist attack? They write. Fired? They write.
Broke an arm? They write with the other arm.

If you ask me what I would do if I lost my right arm
(I'm a rightee), my response would be writing with my left
arm. That's called adapting. It doesn't change my
practice.

Do you know this tip is very important? It's the first
and only rule in planning your time. Because it's not a
rule. You make the rules.

All the "short sessions are great" and "have some
privacy" are under its umbrella. If you know you can't
focus on evenings, you will know to change your writing
time. If you know that you loathe planning and outlining,
you'll find an easier way—maybe a template—to help
you out.

Don't rely on the first timeplan you create for your
book. It won't always work to the letter. You should be
willing to adapt to suit your needs. But do not jeopardize
your writing time.

4. Sketch Your Idea

How do you begin planning your book idea? Note
that it's not planning a book. It's strictly planning your
idea, which I prefer calling sketching your idea.

Do you begin with outlining as inspiration strikes you? Or you don't even give a hoot about planning or outlining?

When you have a book idea, you should first check whether there's a market available for it or not. Check Chapter 6 for how to generate and validate your idea.

I'm going to assume you've done that, that you've also curate topics you'll be covering in your book. If so, what next?

Sketching out your idea. Some call it **the brain dump.**

What is a brain dump?

You pour everything you know or want to cover about your idea on paper or a word processor.

I like doing this on paper because it gives me creative freedom, including free hand co-ordination of everything that goes onto the page.

The benefits of sketching an idea are:

- You see everything your brain has stored about your idea.

- Even if you forget any of the ideas, it's there on the page for you. If an idea strikes you, I recommend you to take a pen and notepad, and sketch the idea as it comes to you. This is to capture the ideas. Who knows, it may be your bestselling book idea.

- You see your book's skeleton.

Plan, Research, and Outline Your Nonfiction Book in a Day

- You figure out what you need to research. You'll discover that your brain doesn't store all information. You need to go get some.

- You figure out what you need to cover that isn't on paper.

- It's usually good for producing a good outline, which will likely serve as your book's table of content.

You may be wondering how all the above benefits are possible. How on earth would scribbling on paper or on my computer help me write a better outline? First, see the below pictures. The first is my idea sketch while the second is the final outline.

district 9110, nigeria

PLANNING

What is planning?
What isn't planning?
What's the difference between planning and outlining?
How do I plan my book?
What do I use to plan my book?
When do I plan my book?

RESEARCHING

What is research? What is researching?
When should I research my book? Do I even need to research?
What are research routines? Should I research my book before, or while writing my book?
What should I do when the need for research arises while writing?
How do I know that my researching is turning into an excuse or procrastination?
Where should I research my book? Physical places or internet?
What do I research for my book?
How do/Ways to research my book?

OUTLINING

What is outlining?
Should I outline or not?
What should I use to outline my book?
How do I outline my book?
What are the methods I can use to outline my book?

Plan, Research, and Outline Your Nonf

Part 1: Introduction
Chapter 1: Dear Reader
Chapter 2: Introduction
Chapter 3: Your Why
Chapter 4: The #1 Habit That Makes All The I

Part 2: Pre-planning Stage
Chapter 6: The #2 Elements of A Bestselling :
Chapter 7: How to Create A Compelling Title

Part 3: Planning Your Book
Chapter 8: Introduction to Planning Your Book
Chapter 9: How to Plan Your Book

Part 4: Researching Your Book
Chapter 10: Introduction to Researching Your Book
Chapter 11: What to Research
Chapter 12: How to Conduct Research on Your B...

Now, you would agree with me that there's no way I would have written an outline like that had I chosen to write the outline first. But as I learned more about this book and added more topics, the outline improved with it.

Here are three ways you could sketch your idea:

1. Question Method

This method is easy. You write out questions your potential reader will likely be asking him/herself while reading your book, which is what I did with my sketch above. It doesn't have to compete with an architect's technical drawing. I call it sketch because it's an overview of your idea.

Checking my dictionary here, the word "sketch" means...

> *...a drawing that is done quickly without a lot of details. Artists often use sketches as a preparation for a more detailed painting or drawing.*

If artists could use a sketch to prepare for a detailed drawing, why shouldn't you sketch your idea in preparation for writing?

Let's assume you want to write a book on creating a self-hosted WordPress blog. Questions your readers may have could be:

1. What is a self-hosted blog?
2. What is the difference between a self-hosted blog and wordpress.com and blogger.com?
3. Where do I host my blog?
4. How do I choose a good hosting company?
5. How much does a hosting account cost?
   ...and so on.

That alone could take a part called "Introduction to Self-hosting Your Blog." Do you see how it helps get to an outline? But if you just attack the page at once and pour out an outline, you reduce your chance of following your project through to the end.

2. Circles on Page

As the title suggests, you draw circles on a page and write topics you want to cover in them. You can link them together. You can draw smaller circles near to a circle and connect them to a bigger one.

The main idea is that you try to organize the ideas as you scribble them. The circles-on-page sketch for this book look like this:

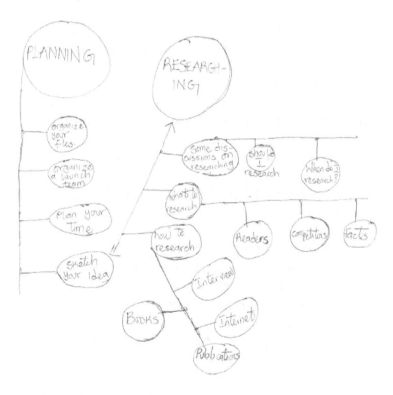

3. List method

Here, you'll lists out topics you want to cover, but not in a particular order. In fact, items on the list may belong to a subtopic category. Don't worry. Just get everything in your brain down on the page.

People love lists, and I believe you love how succinct a list is. That's because we now scan everything.

We scan web pages, we scan books, we scan brochures, we scan catalogs, we scan emails—practically everything. We only pay attention to what we want to pay attention to and what does a fantastic job of holding our attention.

In this case, that would be your list. You should focus on every item on it—there's a 50-50 probability that some items aren't meant to be there. And there's a higher chance that you haven't written all you wanted to or should write.

If I take on the book about self-hosted blog, my list would look like this:

1. What a self-hosted blog is.
2. The difference between wordpress.com, wordpress.org, and a self-hosted blog.
3. How to choose the right web hosting company.
4. Why you should use a self-hosted blog.
5. The cost of registering a self-hosted blog and which hosting company to choose.
6. Free responsive WordPress themes to get you started.

It's straight from the top of my head, but you see the difference between the question version and this version. Although this method can still work out for you, you should consider using the question method.

It will help you while writing your book. If you put a list of questions in front of you, what you write will be different to what you'll write, were you to use a list of headings. This is because it feels like your readers are the ones asking you the questions, and your job is to answer it. You'll only know it will work for you if you try.

5. Determine What You Need to Research

Whether you need to confirm a fact or research for information, you can't do without researching. It's not optional; it's required.

A lot of authors, particularly pantsers, think they can do without it. Probably at the beginning of the project. An idea strikes them, they ruminate a little on it and jump before the computer to start punching keys. Such authors don't realize that the human brain doesn't store all the information humans would have loved to store.

Think of it this way. Your brain tries to store every happening, every single day. It also stores information you don't need frequently like your friends' names, your birthdate, the name of your school, all that. The human brain, though functions like a massive drive, chooses information to store. Maybe by the order of importance.

But today, you don't need to whack your memory until it crashes. (Although, that's certainly disastrous.) The internet is there for you, you have a computer with gigabytes of memory space, and you have physical journals. You should transfer the weight of the information your brain can't handle into any of those mediums.

Have Journals

Not just a normal journal where you record what you feel like. Different journals. For example, you can have an idea journal, email subject swipe file, sales copy formulas in a swipe file, book description templates, etc. They'll save you searching time on the internet.

Now this is where the human brain is good at saving bits of information, something I would call a metadata. Maybe you had written something about writing emails in your journal, your brain might not remember what you've actually written about, but would surely recall that you did write something about it. What's left for you is just to search your journals and there you have it. Sometimes, your brain would store more information about the topic, like where you saved it on your computer, or where you've written it among the documents on your desk, or a unique incident when you were writing it.

You Don't Have to Research Everything

Do you suddenly feel that you have to research your butt off or have a massive journal before you can successfully pull it off? Of course not. What you'll be researching are simply:

- **Your readers.** It's prudent to spend time reading about your readers and getting inside their head.

You should be able to describe your readers as if you knew them from birth. If you can, you'll be able to align with their dreams, validate their fears, give them hope, and convince them that you're the right person—maybe the only person—who can solve their problem.

For more information, check Chapter 11.

- **Your competition.** Would you want your book to be just like any other book out there? Or worse, terrible than the average book?

  If you don't know what your competitions are doing, you won't be able to compete properly. Is that guy just listing out items in his book? Why not explain it. Are they just supporting their book with worksheets? Why not create a course for your own book.

  The goal is not to compete as if you're racing, but to stand out. That is, to be unique and still cater to your customers' need.

  For more information on researching your competitors, check Chapter 11.

- **Facts.** I've said earlier on that you can't do without verifying something in your book, maybe on the internet or in libraries or even from people. In fact, if you don't do any research for your book, it's probably mediocre.

Authors think about facts when their ears sniff the word "research." It depends on the balance you put on a number of facts and competition you research, as well as your readers.

Some books need more facts more than others do. Some need more of researching readers and competition. Some just need more of either of researching readers and researching competition. As an author, you only can decide which one your book needs the most.

If you've done much of researching your readers and competitors before, then you only have to focus on getting the facts in your book right. Even to the least noticed.

For more information on researching facts for your book, check Chapter 11.

6. Create an On-the-go Kit

In other words, organize your materials. You may need to put all your research files where you'll be able to access it easily, such as your travel backpack while traveling, etc. You don't need this for your system because all you have to do is click the icon of whatever application you want to use on your desktop.

With physical things, it may get frustrating. Some of the things you may need to keep where you'll be able to find it easily are:

- Your pen and notepad.
- Dictionary.
- Research files.
- Index cards.

Final Thoughts on Planning Your Nonfiction Book

You're the one to decide what level of planning your book needs. If you know planning may turn into procrastination, then set a deadline for the planning phase.

You should know that planning your book is turning into an excuse or procrastination if:

- You're taking too long, like a week.
- You're planning a part of your book *over and over again.*
- All you're doing is thinking about your book.

Your instinct will tell you if the planning phase is getting too long. But you should recognize that at once if you notice any of the above symptoms.

Planning your book shouldn't take you more than hours, a day at most. Because it evolves as you write your book. At least, you should plan these four things:

1. Organize your files and documents for easy access.
2. Sketch your idea to capture everything you know about the subject.
3. List out what you need to research so that researching would be much better and easier.
4. Plan your time so that you know what you need to do and when, and be able to visualize your progress.

I assure you that if you do that, you've already sailed through the hardest part of the process. It doesn't matter if you can't easily find your laptop or notepad, what matters is to get the word down on paper to meet up to your goal.

The "How to Plan Your Nonfiction Book" Worksheet

For planning your book, I've made a worksheet to help you plan your book. This process should take you an hour or so. At most, a day. Remember that perfectionism is your enemy. You can still tweak your plan as you go on.

You can get the worksheet at the back of this book.

PART 4

RESEARCHING YOUR BOOK

Chapter 10

Introduction to Researching Your Book

What is research?

Now that you've planned your book, it's time to fulfill one of the tasks you promised yourself that you'd do. If you've planned your book using the worksheet that you'll find at the end of this book, then you should have a list containing what you want to research.

Usually, the list contains what you don't know and what you're not sure of about your book topic.

Research is inevitable in the book writing process. You need research every step of the way. Maybe you want to know your readers more like the back of your palm or you want to know what your competitors are doing so that you can zag while they zig. It's all about researching the right way and implementing unique ideas.

According to The Longman Dictionary of Contemporary English, research means:

- ...a serious study of a subject, in order to discover new facts or test new ideas.

- ...the activity of finding information about something that you are interested in or need to know about.

- ...to study a subject in detail, especially in order to discover new facts or test new ideas (i.e. investigate).

- ...to get all the necessary facts and information for something.

All of the above describes research with verbs such as **study, discover, test, find,** etc. That means you could research about anything. For example, you could study a person; you could discover new techniques and test to validate it; you could hunt for your ideal readers. So, research doesn't mean finding facts alone.

Plan, Research, and Outline Your Nonfiction Book in a Day

Here's what Wikipedia(https://en.wikipedia.org/wiki/Research) has to say about research:

> Research comprises *"creative work undertaken on a systematic basis in order to increase the stock of knowledge of humans* [including your readers and competitors], *culture* [that is, trends], *and society, and the use of this stock of knowledge to devise new applications* [that is, using the knowledge you get from the research to do wonderful things such as writing your book]. *It is used to establish or confirm facts* [for example, I argued that research is not only looking for information, as I also did in the planning section], *reaffirm the results of previous work* [a simple documentation of result should explain this], *solve new or existing problems* [as I'm doing now], *support theorems, or develop new theories.*

Here's also what *Merriam-Webster* also has to say about research:

> *A careful study that is done to find and report new knowledge about something. The activity of getting information about a subject.*

A lot of writers think they just have to find facts to use in their book. But wait? Isn't fact what we research?
Not entirely facts. If you say facts, in what context? Facts about your book idea? (That's also a fact.) Facts about your readers?

Facts on the book topic are what some writers think they only have to research. If you also believed that, now is the time to shed and throw it away. Because you need to do research. Maybe a lot.

Don't freak out, I have created a worksheet to make the process easier. If you know what you're doing and what you're looking for, all the research and planning process shouldn't take more than a couple of hours. A day, at most. And that's if you don't even have the time like most full-time writers do.

I don't believe in a lot of research for your book. To me, much of what you need should be coming straight from your head—your experience, what you learned, what worked for you, and even some anecdotes to create a bonding between your readers and you.

Do I need to research?

Short answer: yes, yes.

Long answer: You absolutely have to research, but not everything. As you read along in this book, you'll find that you need to research your readers, information you'll use in your book, and books on your topic.

But it doesn't have to be everything.

Maybe you already know what to write. Let's even say you can write a whole book without looking for anything about it. Or let's assume that you're writing a personal account, a memoir. You don't need to find information about your life, but you need to research about the memoir market, you have to check out other memoirs, you have to analyze their book covers, sales copy, even the content.

So, whether you're writing about your old grandma or a book about brain discectomy, you have to look for something in relation to it.

When should I research my book?

This concerns a lot of writers out there (me included), and they have to decide when to do it. You can't really decide the times you want to research because you have no control over when the occasion you'll need it arises.

That said, there's no time you research your book that isn't good. It doesn't show on your book. You can choose to research…

1. Before you write your book.

This is, in my opinion, is good. You should try all you could to research something about your book before you write a word. For example, I Google articles on planning a book, but many of them leaned toward outlining. None talked about other things you have to plan.

And I had to argue that planning goes more than that. If I'd done nothing before writing my book, I wouldn't have discovered that, and maybe would have ended up writing something slightly similar to the articles out there.

Watch out for procrastination. It's very easy to be seduced into the world of researching your book. Many writers love it, and I believe you also do. But the problem about researching is coming back to the keyboard after some time.

If you're going to start your book after three days and you find yourself still researching on Day 5, you're probably procrastinating.

You should know that you're procrastinating if you spend a long time researching but didn't write a word. Usually, your instinct will tell you that you're just fooling around looking for the same information from different sources.

It's normal. In fact, it happens to all writers. It's like preparing to go to war, only that there's no death or injury involved. You know that if you don't prepare as much as you can, you may be preparing yourself for failure, i.e. death, in the case of a real war.

So, writers count that death as a failure in writing, too. "What if I run into a case where I need information that I have to research? Won't I lose flow and forget all the genius of words I'm about to write?" I know how it feels not to be able to write further because of a silly research. Trust me, I'm not exempted.

We'll discuss that later on, but the most important thing is to begin writing your book. From the first word to the first sentence, to the first paragraph, to the first section. That's how you go.

2. While writing your book.

You may find that you need much research while writing your book, especially if you're writing a "how-to" or technical book. That's fine, and you should do that. But be wary of letting writer's block set in.

Researching instead of writing can sway you away from continuing writing your book. You'll tell yourself that you'll come back to your book and that you just need to scan a book or web page.

As said earlier, getting back to the keyboard is difficult and it matters much to the progress of your book. I don't know which is harder: beginning your book or getting back to continue writing it.

When you want to begin your book, you have the feeling that you may be missing something; that you don't want to go unprepared to the blank screen; that you don't want to do any research while writing your book. When you've begun your book, researching may make you feel that there's a lot of information to gather; that it's like investing 10 hours researching to write just a page of your book; that it will take years before you finish it.

You're the one to make a choice, of course, but don't let it intimidate you.

Watch out for researching more than you write.

3. After you finish your first draft.

You may prefer researching after draft your book, or even after finishing the publishable draft of your book. That's okay if it is for you. But you should avoid, as much as you can, leaving facts in your book unverified.

That little task can pile up into another couple of hours of work. The solution is to check everything as you write your book. This is where researching as you write comes into play; it's not meant to research a complicated subject—that should've been done before writing a word or you should probably set aside a time to research it.

Watch out for leaving all the little facts unverified until you finish your book.

That brings us to the next section.

What should I do when I need information while writing?

This happens a lot, as I said. It's as simple as it can get: **you leave a note for yourself.**

If you're writing in a word processor, you can bold the note, change the text color, and make it larger. Personally, I bold the texts, increase the font size to 20 points, and encircle the text in a block parenthesis, just as below:

> yourself.
>
> If you're writing in a word processor, you can bold the note, change the te and make it larger. Personally, I bold the texts, increase the font size to 20 poi encircle the text in a block parenthesis, just as below:
>
> **[Insert picture of leaving note here.]**
>
> This is because changing the color of the text makes it more difficult to ge writing flow. With keyboard shortcuts, I can bold the words (Ctrl+B) and increa

This is because changing the color of the text makes it more difficult to get back my writing flow. With keyboard shortcuts, I can bold the words (Ctrl+B) and increase the font size (Ctrl+shift+< for decrease or Ctrl+shift+> for increase).

Watch out for vagueness. It can be frustrating to remember which image or information you want to insert in place of the note. Don't give yourself a vague note like, "Insert image here" or "Insert info here."

Make the text specific like, "Insert image about [what you're writing about]" or "This is where I'll put the information on [what the section you're writing in is about]."

Don't also forget to make the font size bigger. It draws your attention, even if you don't bold it. My replacement goes easy-peasy when I search for either half of the block parenthesis. It shows all the places I've used it, but I use it for leaving notes to myself mostly.

How to know that your research is turning into an excuse or procrastination

I hinted on this a while back, but I want to talk more about it.

1. Repeated Verification

Checking the same thing repeatedly but from different sources is the first feeling that sneaks into a writer's mind while researching. It's a feeling of fear.

As human beings, we don't want to miss out on anything. We think there are more facts to extract from the next material we read. Most times, it's a rehearsal of the old materials.

Maybe you don't agree with what you found in a material. It's okay. It happens, but you should have probably observed that the topic you're researching is controversial. Opinions only matter in that kind of space.

You shouldn't be hunting for the one material that will align with your theory. You should, however, move on, and write your opinion. Beware of speaking at your reader.

Also, if you find yourself reading and re-reading about a specific thing, you should mind the amount of time you spend researching. Let's say you're looking for how to format your print book cover for CreateSpace and you found an article on it, you shouldn't read and re-read until you're blue in the face; you should go try it for yourself. If you keep reading, you won't understand some part of the process.

2. Slow Overall Progress

In the worksheet you'll find at the end of this book, there's a section where you write whatever you research about. As you finish reading about each, you should tick them off. If you find your progress slow, then you should check if you're just obsessing about that particular subject.

Anything that causes you to stop writing, but doesn't help you write better is a barrier to your writing.

Is research good for your work? Yes, even necessary. But if that's all you do for two weeks because you want to write a 20-page book, then research has become a barrier to your writing a book that you can finish in two hours.

Chapter 11

What to research

Now that you've known the basics of researching your book, what should research? Is there a worksheet that can make the work faster?

Yes, there is a worksheet that can make the work a little faster for you, but it still boils down to knowing what you want to research and having the ability to discern and choose whatever you want.

The three things you should research are:

1. Readership.

You want people to buy your book. You want them to read it. You want your book to help those people. Every author wants that, too. But you could stand out if you take the time to understand your readers.

In other words, you'll feel a deep connection to them. You'll be able to encourage them, justify their failures, allay their fears, confirm their suspicions, and most importantly, help them solve their problems.

Readers are also people like you. When describing your readers, you should use specific qualities to make them stand out.

For example, saying that your readers are authors looking to publish easily isn't going to be effective than saying that your readers are young writers who probably don't know where to start, don't have a fortune at their disposal, and don't have enough time to learn by guessing.

2. Facts.

I've been giving you facts from the beginning of this book and I'll still be giving you facts until the last chapter of this book.

But in the craft of writing, there is information you have to look for, no matter the genre you write. And those are the information you'll be using in your own book.

It may be just a paragraph, a sentence, or even a phrase. The most important thing is that you look for correct information and give it to your readers in the right order.

For example, if you want to tell your readers how to register on a website, you may not know the actual process. To solve that problem, you should go register on that website and record how you did it. Then you'll be able to show them easily.

3. Competition.

If you want your book to stand out among thousands of books out there, you'll want to "spy" on your competitors. You need to know what they're doing, how they're doing it, when they're doing, and with what they're doing it.

That only comes into play when you go researching about them.

So, where are your competitors? How exactly should you research about them?

Let's take the three one by one.

1. READERSHIP.

This is the first thing you want to research about your book. If nobody would read what you'll be writing, then why write it at all?

At this stage, you'll want to know the **fears of your readers, their problems, and how you can help solve it for them.**

First, you need to know who you'll be writing for.

Who are your readers?

Giving your potential readers a breathing ability will make you understand how to solve their problems. You also need to be specific about their avatar because that'll help you approach them nicely. In other words, that'll help you write a good copy for them.

So you should then ask yourself questions like:

- What gender are my readers? (Fortunately, you don't have control over this except if your topic targets a specific gender e.g. weight loss for women.)

- What are their greatest fears? People have fears, too, and that may be the reason they're coming to you. Common fears that your readers might have are:

  o Fear of failure.
  o Fear of rejection.
  o Fear of missing out.
  o Fear of not knowing.
  o Fear of obscurity.
  o Fear of looking stupid.
  o Fear of feeling inadequate.
  o Fear of embarrassment.
  o Fear of being boring.
  o Fear of pain.

What urgent problems do they have?

Believe it or not, you're in this writing business because you want to solve an urgent problem for someone. Otherwise, you're writing for yourself, and I say, "*Bon voyage.*"

But if you know what you're doing and you want people to read your books, you have to solve people's problem.

Take the fiction writers, for example. They are solving a problem of lack of entertainment. They wield words and they control people's emotion—people laugh, cry, fear, get angry, and even toss their Kindle out of the window. That's fine for them.

For you, you want to minimize entertainment. The people reading your book don't want entertainment; they want answers, solutions, and easier life.

Imagine someone reading a weight loss book and all the book does is jabber about the horror of being fat and the disadvantages of not being slim. Readers will get angry and move to the next book. And if the next book does the same thing, they pass it and may go shoot evil aliens on Xbox.

Write a problem-solving book and, in the act, entertain your readers. Solution to the problem first, while entertainment comes second, except, well, if entertainment is the solution.

Your answer to this question should be succinct and not more than a paragraph. For example, my answer would be:

> My readers, who're young writers, don't know where to go after getting their ideas or are confused as to what to do. They ask themselves,

"Should I start planning, researching, or outlining my book?"

Short and to the point. Here, it clearly tells me that I want to help my readers plan, research, and outline their book. Maybe most of them could use another "how-to-write-a-book" book in writing their book, but the urgent problem here is getting a complete outline of their book, which by then writing should be easier and most of them would be able to proceed.

To answer this question:

- Think of your readers. Remember that you profiled your readers. In your profile, there should be at least a problem connecting you to them.

- Ask yourself what attracted you to them in the first place. For example, I was drawn to young writers because I'm also a young writer and I know what their struggle would be like.

- Ask yourself what specific thing you can help them with right now. For example, I can help them outline their book and I'm doing so.

Can you solve those problems? How?

This is the question that could make or break your book. Simply put, you should ask yourself, "Can I solve [insert those problems here]?"

For example, mine would be:

Plan, Research, and Outline Your Nonfiction Book in a Day

"Can you really help young writers plan, research, and outline their book?"

You should know my answer by now and I choose to solve it by writing a book.

How will you reach them?

If you don't already have a host of audience waiting for your next product, then you have to pen where you'll go look for your ideal readers.

In fact, here's where planning your book is important. You can organize your readers before you even write a word. That will show you that people want your solution. Your ideal readers will tell you whether they want it or not.

Here are mediums you could use to reach them:

Websites/blogs.

Having your own author platform today seem to be the most important kickstart of an author's career. Your website and blog will serve as your brand and a platform for communicating with your readers.

For more on building your author platform, check out Shelly Hitz's *9 Strategies to Build and Grow Your Author Platform.*

Email marketing.

Today, before you go too far in your writing career, the best advice people can give you (even I) is to build your email list. The logic is simple: if

Amazon and other eBook retailers close up shop, you'll be able to adapt. You'll talk directly with your readers and continue your writing journey.

You can start building your email list without a dime. MailChimp.com has a free plan up to 2,000 subscribers.

Public speaking.

Public speaking is also one of the ways you can attract your readers. With the aid of your author platform, the audience you spoke to will be able to find you, join your list, and buy your books.

Memberships and affiliations.

If you belong to a membership site, you can connect with your readers there, too. Most membership sites usually have a forum. If you're helpful there, people will start to notice you.

Media e.g. newspaper column.

If you have a newspaper column, you can advertise your product in your byline.

JV partner.

Joint-venture partners can help you advertise your product to their audience. They may be bloggers or authors like you.

Paid ad e.g. banner ad, sponsored post/review.

Many blogs and websites with high traffic do place banner ads on their web pages. You pay for ads like that of Google Adwords' when people click on it.

Bloggers do have a flat rate for a given month.

Word of mouth.

Apart from the word-of-mouth advertising that you do yourself, your subscribers will also help you do it if they like your work.

It works this way. Suppose you have two subscribers and those two subscribers tell two of their friends each and those four new subscribers tell two of their friends each, in no time, you'll see a difference.

Writing conferences.

Writing conferences are designed for two things: to learn and to connect.

You don't have to be a chronic socializer to make this work. Just be polite and professional. A business card will do and free copies of your books, if you have.

Other ways you can connect with your readers are signing a book tour with a publishing company and a blog tour with a blogger.

Where do they hang out mostly?

If they're not on your list, well, you'll need to go find them. And you can only do that if you know where to find them.

Having known the answers to all those questions, you'll find that you now know your readers like the back of your palm.

2. FACTS

As said earlier, writers think they only have to look for facts that will go on the pages. At least, the beginners. But you still have to.

It's required that the facts, no matter how little, should be correct and up-to-date. But what are the things you could research for to make words on the page authentic? Here they are:

People and their culture.

When writing fiction, you can't do without description, especially that of characters. But in nonfiction, we research about people to know them more and be able to refer to them the right way.

I know my readers and that's why I'm referring to them as "Young Writers." I also know that I'm writing for writers who are sometimes known as and called authors, authorpreneurs, etc.

You may not need much of this for writing your book, so you can count it as researching about your book.

Places.

You don't need to do this in all nonfiction. For example, I don't need to look for information about anywhere because of this book, but you may need to if you're writing about a regional subject like cheap hotels in Vatican, then you have to look for information on it.

Instructions and how-tos.

Have you noticed how nonfiction book titles used to have action words, especially in the subtitles? This book contains three: **plan, research, and outline.** That's because people are looking for something they can do to solve their problem.

Are you writing a book on weight loss? Readers want to know how to lose weight. Or a book on making money? Readers want to know how to make money. Even while reading books about introversion, readers are looking for how they can cope in life with extroverted people. Introverts usually ask themselves, "How can I cope with this people? Is there anything I can do blend into the pack?"

So, we're all looking for something tangible to grasp in nonfiction books. You should ask yourself questions like:

What part do I explain something in this book? For example, I explain how to plan a nonfiction book in this book, how to research it, as well as outlining it. So, you could say that the how-to parts I researched are:

How to plan a nonfiction book.
How to research a nonfiction book.
How to outline a nonfiction book.

You don't have to research everything. You should only research what you aren't sure of or don't know

If you find yourself asking, "Hey, how do I teach them to plan their book?" go look for information about it. Or, preferably, go do it and record how you did it.

Scientific and technical concepts.

Imagine I want to teach you how to use HTML to format your book descriptions and I don't know *no* jack about it, what do I do?

Of course, I'll go look for it and practice. I'll also do the same thing if I'm writing about the psychology of anything. You know, scientific stuff.

Statistics.

How many blogs are on the internet? Honestly, I can't answer that question.

"I think I remember it's 152 million. Or is it 172? Oh yes, I remember reading somewhere that it's 200 million this year?"

If you find yourself doing that, go look for the statistics you're looking for. This also applies to taxes, payroll, anything numbers.

The Few Things You'll Mostly Have to Research

I don't believe in doing a lot of research work. In fact, the lesser and smarter the work, the better it is. Below are a few things that you'll most likely only have to research:

- Statistics. For example, how many blogs are there in the world?
- Websites. For example, sites that add more value to your content.
- Stories, usually to back up your claim.
- Instructions and how-tos. For example, how to convert an MS Word file to Kindle MOBI.
- Reading to get a clear idea and further clarification of a smaller topic, which is inevitable if you'll be searching for the content not pouring them down on the page.
- Articles that explain more of what you're writing about.

3. COMPETITION

To give your book a chance of survival, you have to make it stand out from a host of books out there. You have to see what's going on, first.

After all, you don't want your book to mimic some similar books. Once you know those books, you want to know what they're doing and how they're doing it.

I should also tell you that researching for competition is not only researching about books. As an author, one of your competitors may be a website or even a software. Once you analyze it as explained below, you should know your chance of making headway with that book.

Here are the questions you should ask yourself while researching about your competitors:

How many competitors are there?

This is the first thing you should consider doing whenever you want to analyze your competition. You may want look for the number of authors writing in your space.

For example, I'm writing for young writers. There's a possibility that someone out there is also doing the same. But people are already out there writing about self-publishing to its general audience. So, to stand out, I choose a specific audience—young writers.

Thousands of authors are out there writing about writing and self-publishing. That is a good sign. A saturated market means:

1. There's going to be fierce competition. Follow general trends and see your book buried in obscurity.

2. You have to stand out. Because of the fierce competition, you need to stand out. You need to narrow down the audience you're targeting so that the competition can admit you.

Also, nobody writing about a topic means:

1. There's no market at all. The reason you find nobody writing on that subject is that people are not interested in it. No other explanation.

2. It may be a potential market. But nobody can tell when it's going to become a market for real. That means you won't earn a dime from there even if you buy the most expensive

course on writing and spend thousands of dollars on advertising.

There's no such thing as a moderate market. It's either a market with fierce competition or no market at all. It's only when you target a specific audience that the market now possesses a moderate competition.

Who are your competitors? What are the competing books?

There are probably hundreds, if not thousands, of books that will be competing against your book. You're not to record all of them, but the bestsellers. By doing this, you're raising the standard for your book, but not overwhelming yourself.

The main goal is to plot your book's chance of survival without putting pressure on yourself.

So right now, in the worksheet provided, write at least ten books on your subject that on bestselling categories.

What is the quality of the content of those books? Book covers, blurbs, content, formatting, etc.?

Not all books out there have something unique to them, but you want to know why the books you have written in your worksheet are bestsellers or at least on bestselling categories.

What's common with their book covers? How do they format their book description? How is the actual content of the book?

You could rate each book on a scale of one to ten. One point may be for cover, another for the blurb, another for the content, another for reviews, etc. Just do what works best for you here and rate the books.

What are the different price points of those books? Free, $.99, $2.99?

As you check the quality of those books, you should check their price, too. How much do you see a 50-page ebook priced? What about a hundred page book?

Now let's say the 50-page book is priced at $2.99 and the 100-page book st $.99. You should ask yourself why. Is the author trying to attract customers for other products like courses and software at the backend? How about the 50-page book author? Is he trying to make more revenue?

This philosophy can help you a lot. For example, if you're using your book as an incentive to attract leads to other products at the backend and you see major bestselling books priced at $.99, then there's nothing bad in pricing your book also at $.99.

Because these books are bestsellers, not just the ones licking dust on page 20 in the search result, and the authors maintained the system because it worked for them.

On the same worksheet, write the different prices of the books in the price column.

What are the quantities? Word count, book pages? And at what price?

On Amazon and other eBook retailing sites, if quality is king and promotion is queen, then quantity is both prince and princess. Readers will discover your books if you keep publishing more.

Because of that, quantity is also one of the things you should consider along as you research your book. This will let you know the quantities different authors are publishing on that subject.

For example, if you keep seeing a variation of 50 to 100 pages book in the bestseller list on your subject, there's a reason for that. That means, if you plan to write a 23-page book, you're just fooling yourself.

Also, it will make you determine topics you should add to your book. Most importantly, it lets you choose which quantity you want to publish.

How can you stand out?

Now that you've reached this stage, you can then plot your own uniqueness. Is there anything you wish the books had touched on? How can you surpass the quality? Or do something unique?

Will designing enticing book covers make you stand out? Or writing attention-grabbing, emotion-driven blurbs? Or writing the content in simple diction as opposed to the *"professorial"* tone of others?

All-time bestselling books also receive one-star reviews. Go check it out. Read from the most critical reviews, first. By the time you start reading the one-star reviews, you'll have covered most of them.

Now proceed to the five-stars. You can skip one-liner reviews. The first couple of reviews will be the most helpful review. Read them. By now, you'll have known what most readers dislike about a book.

That's your cue. You should emulate what readers say they like and avoid what they say they don't like.

Chapter 12

How to conduct Research for Your Book

You probably think you can only research your book through the internet because a lot of information is now available online for free. There are courses online similar to a college diploma, floods of eBooks everywhere, and, of course, millions of websites with free content. Information is available for free almost everywhere you turn.

But there's more to researching. The internet doesn't and will not provide every (or detailed) information. (Its job is to provide any content, after all.) So, how do you research? What should you do because you want your book's content to be correct, verified, and up-to-date?

Below are ways you could research your book.

1. Interviews.

Interviews are vital in obtaining the information you can only get face-to-face. It can help with writing a historical book.

You could also interview to get people's opinion in your book, say, on a controversial topic like, "Would you outline your book before writing or not?" or "Why should writers outline?" You'd lean on a side rather than writing from a neutral point, if you write about that yourself.

You can post the interview in your book in its entirety, with the interviewee's permission.

Also, you can use interviews to provide a case study for a particular subject or technique. For example, if I want to write about young writers' success stories, I'll opt for asking them how they did it, what they did, their mindset, and external factors that determined their success.

You could use interviews to:

1. Research information the internet can't provide you.

2. Curate people's opinion about a controversial topic.

3. Do a case study about a specific people.

But why interview people?

1. To get facts.
2. To add a perspective to your book.
3. To get other people's opinion.
4. To connect with your readers and interviewees more.
5. To use as a promotion strategy.

The benefits of interviewing people for your book, among others, are:

1. You build your authority in a niche.
2. You add other people's voice to your book.
3. Your interviewees provide you an additional content.
4. You build relationships with your interviewees.
5. You learn a thing or two as you ask your interviewees questions about your topic.
6. You connect with your fanbase.
7. Your fans know that you're a human because you'll share your vulnerabilities.
8. You expand your reach as you interview other authority figures in your industry.

Here are the three ways to interview someone:

1. Face-to-face.

This is, by far, the best way of conducting an interview. Seeing your interviewee(s) face-to-face gives you some advantages over other mediums. For example, you decipher emotion and its message while interviewing physically. Otherwise, you wouldn't get anything.

You should conduct an interview in person if:

- Your interviewee has gained a reputation of lying. ("All liars shall be interviewed in person," I paraphrase Jeff Goins. Check out the real quote here: http://thewritepractice.com/should-you-be-interviewing-people-in-person-or-by-email/)

- You really want to see someone cry. (That's if the topic you're discussing warrants it.)

- The subject of discussion requires a lot of explanation and descriptions. Something as little as hand gestures can help you understand a sophisticated concept. Still, the interviewee could show you diagrams, charts, and photos in person.

- You're interviewing about a practical subject. I hope you know that interviewing an artist by phone or email just wouldn't cut it? Because you have to use all your five senses to imbibe so much to understand the artist's explanation.

- You don't have much time or aren't patient. In this case, you can tie your bow tie in a haphazard way and chase your interviewee's limousine on a highway in New York.

Goodluck! Interviewing by phone and email takes time. You have to schedule the interview time and both of you have to make the appointment.

2. By phone.

Interviewing by phone is (and should be) the second way you resort to when you want to interview anybody. Because it still gives you a fragment of the emotions you'd otherwise lose if you interview by email.

You can hear the interviewee's voice and, with the powerful emotion a sound can evoke, you judge your interviewee's answers. You can know if they're angry, or if they're happy, or even they hold a safe spot far, far away from any side of an opinion.

You should interview by phone if:

- You don't have a chance to meet the interviewee. People from different continents still interview each other without leaving their front door, because technology has made it possible.

- You aren't awarded an interview in person. Maybe your interviewee was busy or he just doesn't take an interview in person. That's fine. You can propose interviewing him by phone.

3. By email.

This medium of interviewing is (and should be) the last you resort to. Email is a very easy way to reach prospective interviewees. It's available, but it isn't fast. A prospect may take days or even months to reply to an email. Or the email may be left unanswered. It's the slowest medium of interviewing.

But it saves you time. You don't have to chase people in offices or limos. You don't even have to keep a phone appointment. You just send an email and the interviewee replies with an answer.

You should interview by email if:

- You aren't awarded either of interviewing in person or by phone.

- You can't reach your prospects because of glitches in technology. (My internet over here is *kinda* slow. If I try to interview someone via Skype, I know it's *gonna* be a disaster. But emails would be a lifesaver.)

- You have a speaking phobia or are dumb. Seriously, I'm being serious here, well, because it may take three serious in a sentence to prove my point. What if an interviewer is dumb? Interviewing someone in person or by phone would be out of the matter, so he/she has to interview by email.

  Also, some interviewers might be introverts, so they don't have enough courage to approach someone for an interview. In that case, an

email would do because it doesn't require the
interviewer to be with his/her prospects in
person or on phone.

2. Books

Reading books is next to interviewing people.
Because it's not possible to interview every genius on
the planet, but reading books written by those people
you'd have otherwise interviewed is also like interviewing
them. Only that they give you answers to questions they
think or know you'd have.

Nowadays, books are easy to buy or borrow. You
could walk up to your local library and ask for books
about your book's topic. You could also ask **librarians.**
Librarians can point you to books, journals, and
periodicals you can find information about your book
topic. You can also find interesting books to research in
bookstores and on the internet.

3. Publications e.g. Magazines and Newspapers

Newspapers do have columns for a particular
subject like business and investing, dating and
relationship, etc. They can also be a helpful backlist of
advice and opinions on your book topic.

4. Internet

The internet is the most widely used medium for conducting research. It's easy, available, and contains materials you may not even find in libraries and bookstores.

You may also have guessed that I use the internet for researching my books, too. Some of the places to find information to use in your book are:

- Websites e.g. Wikipedia
- Blogs
- Slides e.g. slideshare.com
- Videos e.g. Youtube.com
- eBooks

The Only Medium of Researching You Need and A Word About Documentation

You already know where I'm going. It's the internet. To arrive at your outline in a day, you don't have the luxury of agonizing over every detail you have to find, over every idea you have to absolutely get right, and over the little details you have to expand to make your book look more professional.

You must be time conscious if you want to get things done fast. At length, you could add an interview by email, which probably could get a reply by the time you finish your book, so it's not a good thing. It would probably take a week to read a full-length, 400-page book on the topic you want to write. I believe you don't have the time to scour newspapers for columns and articles on your subject.

Plan, Research, and Outline Your Nonfiction Book in a Day

So, the internet is the only way to get your research done faster if you want to have an outline by the end of a day.

As you research, you may be tempted to record whatever you want to where you also have your ideas sketched out. No, your documentation should be recorded somewhere you can easily access.

PART 5

OUTLINING YOUR BOOK

Chapter 13

Introduction to Outlining Your Nonfiction Book

The "outlining or not" debate has been rampant on the internet lately for a reason: we're all different. What works for me may not work for you. And what works for you may be a total disaster to my writing process.

But in spite of the virtual war between the pantsers (the folks who say they write by the seat of their pants) and outliners, we can remain objective. What exactly do outliners (or planners, if you will) benefit that pantsers don't? What advantages do pantsers have over planners?

The Benefits of Outlining

Outlining, though rejected by others, also have a benefit. Some of them are:

1. Focus.

When you segment and work on your writing with the help of an outline, you'll have a clear focus. You never get lost while writing your book. And even if it does happen, you refer back to your outline and it points you back on track.

You don't have to focus on the overall picture. Instead, you focus on getting a section or chapter done. You may even discover that you say much when you focus only on a section or chapter than when you focus on the overall picture.

Because you may be distracted. You could be passionate about a chapter or a part of your book. You could find yourself brainstorming that chapter or part while writing another, which will slow down your writing.

2. Testing your content.

Outlines help you discover problems like plot holes, not having enough content for a book, etc. Some writers think they have enough content to write a book when, in reality, it's an article or a couple of articles. If you outline before you write it, you'll surely know your content isn't enough.

Also, it lets you arrange your thought in a logical order.

3. You can modify it.

Who said you have to stick to your rough (and first) outline to the letter? Those who know how to adapt could easily modify anything in their outline and move on with their writing. Whatever happens, you can modify and even abandon it. If inspiration happens to strike you, you can forget about your outline for that moment and follow your instinct. Outlines aren't militia rules; they're meant to be guides, like a General's orderly.

4. A sense of flow.

Your writing flows from a chapter or section to the other while writing with an outline. Instead of groping for words, you just have to look at your outline, and then you know what next to write.

5. Can eliminate writer's block.

Writer's block plagues many writers today. They sit at their desk and stare at the blank page instead of attacking it with words the way they wanted to. Writer's block may be:

- I don't want to write now.
- I don't know what to say.

127

- I know what to say, but not how.

Most times, it's the third option. They know that words are dying to escape from them, but they may not know how.

Outlines can help with that. As said earlier, outlines are to be guides, not militant rules. I think the way you outline helps solve the problem. If you write a brief paragraph to yourself, detailing what you want to write for that section, it shouldn't be that hard. For example, it could be:

> *In this section, I'll write about the benefits and shortcomings of outlining a book before writing.*

You may even give yourself a list or a little more detail:

> *In this section, I'll write about the benefits and shortcomings of outlining a book before writing. I've found that outlining helps keep focus, stay on track, overcome writer's block, etc.*

When done well, your outline could practically be telling you what to write next without any problem. It's what I've also done for this book. Refer to Chapter 19 to see how I created an outline that tells me what I wanted to write.

6. Saves you time.

You'll write faster when you use an outline. It helps you stay on track. You don't have to think, "Hey, what's next?" That's the work of your outline.

7. Makes communicating your points easier.

Since outlining a book takes the points you're to
make in logical order, you'll be communicating to your
readers in a logical way.

8. Helps you research aforehand.

Remember how in Chapter 9 we talked about
determining what you need to research? An outline
helps you research those topics before you write
anything. When you take a good look at the outline,
you'll know what chapter, or section or part you don't
know and should research.

The Disadvantages of Outlining

1. Spoils the fun of creativity.

Outlining could make writing boring. Suddenly, you
find that you're tied to the outline. You couldn't explain a
section the way you shouldn't. Instead, you're focusing
on the next one.

Yes, it happens to some and it's fine. For people like
that, they don't have to outline aggressively. A list of
what they're going to cover, laid chapter-by-chapter,
could serve them better.

I've discovered that there's a balance between
outlining and tying oneself to a list of ideas. For each
writer, there's always a balance point. For example, I
don't see myself plotting every character, every scene, if

I were to write a novel, but I might just list everything out with an accompanying short description—a couple of sentences.

So, if you actually see this happening you, you're not an aggressive planner. And yes, it does spoil the fun for a lot of writers.

2. Your outline may not be good for your writing style.

You can outline your book a thousand and one ways, but a thousand out of it may not match your style. So, if you find your writing style stalling after you try outlining, chances are that you've chosen the wrong way of outlining it.

Outlining, if not done right, can wreck havoc to some people's writing.

3. If you change course, your outline, no matter how detailed, is rendered useless.

What's the point of creating an outline that could be subject to change any moment? Of course, no point, except maybe you thought that first outline would be the final outline of your book.

Outlines aren't a set-it-and-forget thing. They evolve as you write, research, and edit your book. So, a writer who thought a first outline would most likely be the final one will be disappointed.

4. You may feel obliged to stick to an outline, which really sucks.

I've felt thus many times. It sucks. After all, I created the outline to follow it. But that's not how outlines should be used. They should be used as a guide.

5. Outlining can take time.

There we go again! Can't I just do some magic and get this thing done in a few hours? Yes, you can. But it's likely not to be the final outline of your book. That's why it takes time to arrive at the final one. Or even an outline that could guide you. That's why some people shy away from outlining.

Again, some writers don't see the wisdom in outlining a short piece, like a blog post. It could take equal time as the writing itself.

So, should you outline or not?

No right or wrong answer for this, but I believe we can all do with outlining. We just have our balance point.

In summary, outlining may not be right for a writer and it may be a lifesaver for another writer.

Chapter 14

Tools for Outlining Your Book

You could use varieties of tools to outline, but using a word processor wouldn't cut it. Especially now that there are tens of tools dedicated outlining. You'd battle styles, paragraphs, indents, etc. if you were to use a word processor. But it can be easier.

The tools you could use to outline your book are below. I've used nearly all of them at a point. I may use some in the future.

1. Pen and Paper

Pen and paper aren't just for technophobic writers. It's good in that you have the freedom to coordinate what goes onto the page and where. You can write in the margins, draw lines, or anything creative to help you along the way.

Using pen and paper also help you avoid staring at a screen all the time, which could lead to skipping or misspelling words. It's happened to me once. I wanted to write, "No, especially including mature content." Instead, I wrote, "Yes, especially including mature content." One slight change in a sentence like that alters the meaning.

You wouldn't make a gross mistake as that if you use paper. Sure, your outline won't be perfect the first time around. In fact, you'll tweak it many times as you write, so no need to obsess over the first one.

See the outline for this book on a paper:

Plan, Research, and Outline Your Nonfiction Book in a Day

Plan, Research, and Outline Your Nonf

Part 1: Introduction
Chapter 1: Dear Reader
Chapter 2: Introduction
Chapter 3: Your Why
Chapter 4: The #1 Habit That Makes All The I

Part 2: Pre-planning Stage
Chapter 6: The #2 Elements of A Bestselling :
Chapter 7: How to Create A Compelling Title

Part 3: Planning Your Book
Chapter 8: Introduction to Planning Your Book
Chapter 9: How to Plan Your Book

Part 4: Researching Your Book
Chapter 10: Introduction to Researching Your Book
Chapter 11: What to Research
Chapter 12: How to Conduct Research on Your B...

Also, see the idea sketch I did for this book:

PLANNING

What is planning?
What isn't planning?
What's the difference
between planning and
outlining?
How do I plan my
book?
What do I use to plan
my book?
When do I plan my book?

RESEARCHING   district 9110, nigeria

What is research? What is researching?
When should I research my book? Do I even
need to research?
What are research routines? Should I research
my book before or while writing my book?
What should I do when the need for research
arises while writing?
How do I know that my researching is turning
into an excuse or procrastination?
Where should I research my book? Physical
places or internet?
What do I research for my book?
How do/Ways to research my book?

OUTLINING

What is outlining?
Should I outline or not?
What should I use to outline
my book?
How do I outline my book?
What are the methods I
can use to outline my book?

2. Mind Mapping

Thousands of mind mapping softwares are probably out there, but I use **FreeMind.** It's free and you can download it here:
http://freemind.sourceforge.net/wiki/index.php/Download

A useful software, you could export your mind map to the following file format:

- HTML
- PDF
- SVG
- PNG
- JPEG
- Open Office Document

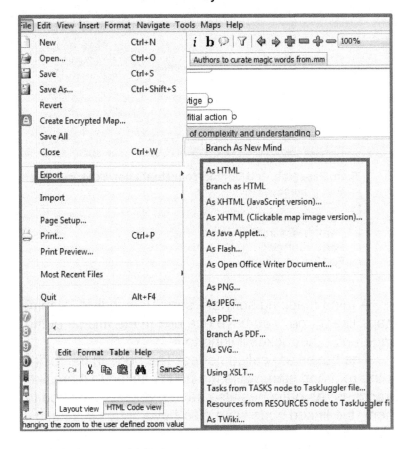

Plan, Research, and Outline Your Nonfiction Book in a Day

You can even copy and paste your mind map from FreeMind to MS Word. It will appear like this:

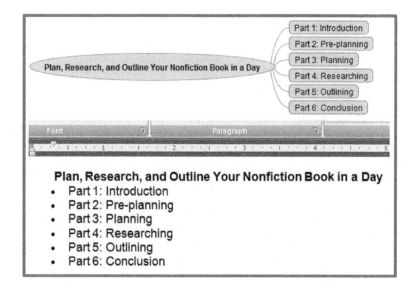

A mind mapping software structures individual mind maps like a tree. You have one box in the middle of the page and other boxes linking to it.

The boxes are called nodes. The node in the middle is the root and stem while the nodes linked to it are like branches. As branches also have branches attached to them, the linked nodes can also have nodes linking to them each.

Unlike a tree, you can cloak the nodes beyond the first layer, and leave only the root and the main branches.

When you open Freemind, it opens a new document just as MS Word and a root node saying, "New Map." Click on it to edit.

To add a branch (known as a child node), right-click on the root node and select "New Child Node." You can add as many branches as you want, but you cannot treat the root node as a branch, so you can't add a sibling node to it as if it were a branch. A sibling node is a box in the same layer as the layer selected.

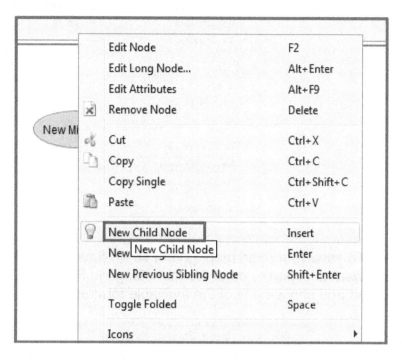

To add another layer of nodes to a node, right click on the node you want to add another layer of nodes to and select "New Child Node." When in edit mode of a node, press the Enter key to save your text and press again to add a sibling node below it.

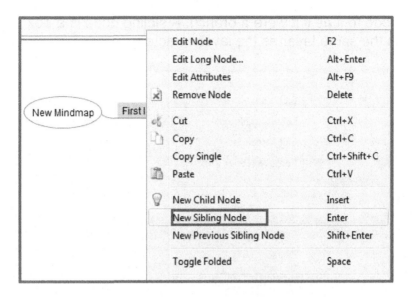

To save your mind map, go to File >> Save as. Or if you want to export to other file formats, go to File >> Export and choose any of the available formats.

3. yWriter6

yWriter6 labels itself as a "Novel Writing Software" but I think it's a beautiful outlining tool. It's structured to record information in Chapters and Scenes. Why? Because novels are written in chapters and/or in scenes, which will serve as an outline. Look at this sample:

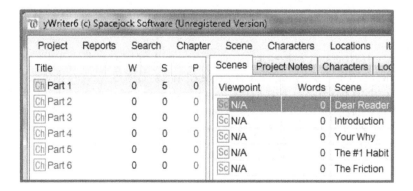

In my case, chapters became different parts of this book and the scenes were the chapters. If you don't want to work by scene, you can use the chapters for its purpose and make different scenes a section of a chapter.

It helps you write better and faster. You select a section and write. What I do is write in MS Word and copy to it. Of course, you could also write in it and copy elsewhere.

You could write in fullscreen mode as well as in floating mode:

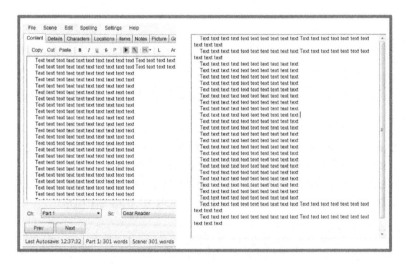

It doesn't take up much space. Last time I checked, the folder I created for a project was 12KB. Even if you enable frequent backups, you have control over which file to keep.

You can download yWriter6 here: http://www.spacejock.com/yWriter6_Download.html

4. Blog post

A blog post also can help outline your book. You can use tags and categories to organize them. It doesn't have to be public, of course. You'll be dealing with it in the backend.

For example, if I were to use a blog post to outline this book, I'd use categories for each part and then the blog post title as the chapter title.

You can also use contents you have on your blog. You can compile it and add necessary parts to it.

Other tools you could use are:

- Scrivener.
- Evernote.
- PowerPoint Slides.
- Sticky notes.

Summary

Here's a recap of what we talked about:

- There's no definite tool for outlining your book. When you think you've found one that best suits you, another one pops into your face.

- Tools you could use to outline your books are:

    o Pen and paper.
    o Mind mapping software e.g. Freemind
    o yWriter6

- Blog posts.
- Scrivener.
- Evernote.
- PowerPoint Slides.
- Sticky notes.

Chapter 15

Arranging Your Outline in the Right Order

As said earlier, outlines evolve as you write, so, you may have to tweak it frequently. (I know that this isn't a writing book, but I want to show you how outlining goes beyond just listing out ideas. I'll show you my outline versions soon.)

You'll want to rearrange your outline if need be, but if you're not careful, it could waste time and lead to writer's block.

I usually modify on paper before tampering with the real outline. For example, I'm writing the "outlining your book" part of this book now, and it comprises of a few chapters. I may want to move things around even in that section.

If you do it that way, you won't have to worry about other parts or chapters of your book. Because as you question the authenticity of the part you're working on, you'll also want to question the authenticity of the overall outline.

That's okay. It means you're now thinking beyond what you were thinking of when you began writing your book. So, quickly get going and finish your first draft.

That said, below are ways you could rearrange your outline:

1. In an Alphabetical Order

You may want to get creative with your writing. Or your readers may have to follow a process starting from acronym A to Z. Arranging ideas in an alphabetical order won't always work. It could only work for you if:

- You're working on a creative piece of writing.

- Readers have to follow your book from A to Z.

2. From the Start of a Process to Finish

This is especially true for *how-to* books. Tutorial books teaching a process have to start from the beginning of the process and then work their way down.

For example, you could outline a part of a recipe book thus:

- Ingredients.
- Method one.
- Method two.
- Method three.

You have to start from the first step of the process: gathering ingredients; then to the end of the third method of preparation. Here's a sample outline of the writing process from start to finish:

- Conceiving an idea.
- Brainstorming.
- Outlining.
- Writing.
- Editing
- Proofreading.

The outline grows beyond that when you include self-publishing or pitching editors.

3. In Logical Order

A book that doesn't have a clearly defined starting point should always flow in logical order. It should make a sense. For example, every piece of writing always has an introduction, a body, and a conclusion. That's the universal logical structure of a book.

Imagine I want to write a book about why you shouldn't patronize vanity publishers, my outline could probably be:

- Introduction.
- What is vanity publishing?
- Why many writers patronize vanity publishers?
- What those writers experienced as a result of patronizing the vanity publishers.
- Why you shouldn't patronize them.
- The alternative to vanity publishers.
- Conclusion.

Now imagine I changed the outline above to this:

- Introduction.
- The alternative to vanity publishers.
- Why many writers patronize vanity publishers.

It doesn't fit together, doesn't make sense that way, and my readers are going to wonder, "What the hell?"

Summary
You don't have to arrange your outline perfectly as you write your book's first draft. But keep in mind that it will help get you the outline you can use for a Table of Contents faster.

To recap, here are the three ways you could rearrange your outline:

1. From A to Z.
2. From the start of a process to the end.
3. In logical order.

Chapter 16

The Book Outline Formula

You could outline a book faster when you use a formula. Here's where you'll use the information you've gathered in chapter 11.

The bunch of research pays off here. You get to use them here to:

- Arrive at a final Table of Contents. I advise you to use this formula when you're done with your book—that is, when you're about to format it. Why? Because moving things around may seem like a lot of work.

While writing your book, I advise you to have a sketched idea on paper where you can arrange the ideas as you write and learn more about your subject.

- Write your book description (the one you could put on Amazon) easily. Now that you've known what your competitors don't address, ways they could do better, and what your readers are dying to pay for, writing a blurb would be much easier, when you put them up in a place where you can see them (with your outline).

  You don't have to rack your brain on the purpose of the book or the value readers will get from it. You just look up at your outline and you start writing your sales letter.

So, what the book outline formula?

TITLE:

SUBTITLE:

AUTHOR'S GOALS WITH THE BOOK:

AUDIENCE (YOUR READERS):

Plan, Research, and Outline Your Nonfiction Book in a Day

URGENT PROBLEMS YOUR READERS HAVE
(that you're solving in your book):

CONSEQUENCE OF THE PROBLEM WITHOUT A
SOLUTION:

BENEFITS READERS WILL DERIVE FROM YOUR
BOOK:

INTRODUCTION

CHAPTER ONE:
    INTRODUCTION:
    SUBHEAD:
      A POINT
      ANOTHER POINT
    ANOTHER SUBHEAD:
      A POINT
      ANOTHER POINT
    CONCLUSION

CHAPTER TWO:
    INTRODUCTION:
    SUBHEAD:
      A POINT
      ANOTHER POINT
    ANOTHER SUBHEAD:
      A POINT
      ANOTHER POINT
    CONCLUSION

CHAPTER THREE:
    INTRODUCTION:
    SUBHEAD:

```
    A POINT
    ANOTHER POINT
  ANOTHER SUBHEAD:
    A POINT
    ANOTHER POINT
  CONCLUSION
```

CONCLUSION

Pretty simplistic, isn't it? Let's take it consecutively. You could adapt this formula and include a brief description of each part. You'll see how I've done mine later in this book. So, let's take each element now.

TITLE AND SUBTITLE

In chapter 7, we talked about how to create an irresistible title. Now's the time to put it here. It can be in the format:

Title: *the long, long, long subtitle.*

GOALS

Write the goals you want to achieve with the book here. Is it gaining more subscribers? Or selling a thousand copies? Or becoming a bestseller? You can also write your strategies here.

READERS

We've discussed how to know more about your
readers in Chapter 11. You can refer back to it for more
details.

Write a sentence or two that best describes your
readers here. For example, the description of a weight
loss reader could be:

> *A nursing mother who spends more time
> caring for her babies, but still wants to lose weight
> at the same time.*

URGENT PROBLEMS

You may have written this in the description of your
readers. In that case, you can omit this part. But it can
be helpful if repetition grabs your attention.

CONSEQUENCE

This is what happens when your readers don't have
a solution to the urgent problem they have. For example,
a fat, nursing mother will end up gaining more weight
and may feel ashamed of her image or may be
humiliated.

For example, the consequence of the problem
above could be:

> *Tendency to gain more weight, if not already
> doing so. Feels ashamed of herself. May be
> subject to humiliation.*

BENEFITS

Finally, this is what your book will help your reader do. You write what happens after you remove your readers' consequences. For example, following the sequence above, the benefit that nursing mother could derive are:

Losing weight instead of gaining more. Has a beautiful image she's proud of. No humiliation.

INTRODUCTION

Your introduction is shaped based on everything above. It is the first thing a reader will read in your book, though, Amazon bypasses that and starts at where it considers the starting of your book, which is usually Chapter One. If there's no labeled chapter, the software guesses the best starting point.

But despite this, do you know what your readers do? They go back. Where? Some, to the Table of Contents. Some, to the cover page. I've done that countless times. So, there's much chance that your readers want to capture everything in your book because they've dedicated a part of their life and their money to it.

But here comes the real question: how do you make the introduction fantastic? How do you make your readers beg for more, which means reading the first chapter? I'm not a pro writer. At least, I don't consider myself one yet. I've done my fair share of "Thank you for downloading this book blah blah blah."

I'm not saying that's a bad way to start a book, but it's what you put in it that matters. So, can we investigate more a little bit? What should go in your introduction?

Plan, Research, and Outline Your Nonfiction Book in a Day

1. A story.

I haven't written the introduction of this book yet, but yes, I'll begin it with a story. Stories have been around for who-knows-how-long. I remember when I was a kid. My dad would take my sisters and me to the roofless top of our house and tell us stories in the night's breeze. I used to be enthusiastic about it.

But don't think people don't love stories anymore, just because you don't feel the same. Stories bond you with your readers. It shows them that you're a human, that you're vulnerable, that you care about their mistakes, their failures, and that you want to erase their pain forever.

In your book, tell the story of how you came about to write your book. Tell them how you failed just like them. Tell them how life would be easier when they apply your solution.

Tell them how angry you were at everybody for not telling you what you're about to tell them. Tell them how you just wish everybody would know about it.

Your readers will love you for it.

2. A problem.

This isn't necessarily a story, but it describes the pain your reader is going through to the point that he/she bought your book. It describes what your readers want to achieve. It describes the enemy they also want to throw a stone.

It lingers in their mind. They would get rid of it at any cost. You could begin with that.

155

3. How the book will benefit them.

Yes, you also don't want to jabber on about your readers' pain. If it continues, they'll start to think, "Hey, I get it, I have that problem. So, what can you do about it now as you promised?"

You silence that voice by telling them where they'll be after reading the book, what they would've achieved, and how happy they would be.

As regarding an outline, what should be present? Because right now, you aren't writing your book yet, you're outlining it. The only exception is if you've written the book already. Then you can go back to the introduction you've written and summarized it in your outline.

Simple: what should be in your outline are elements you want to use. A story? You can write the details down there. Want to start with a problem? Yeah, put a summary of the ever-present nuisance your readers are dying to get rid of.

So, let's see how an outline for an introduction would look like. Imagine you want to write a book on Weight Loss, here are examples of what can go in the introduction:

Introduction
My story of losing 50 pounds in a week.
Humiliation as an obese.
You're reading this book because you want to lose weight.
I'll teach you to eat fat and lose weight as you do so.

See that? Succinct. Details in outlines don't have to be a list either. It could be in a sentence form. For example:

Introduction
Oh, how I was happy when I finally lost 50 pounds. The story of how I lost weight while doing no exercise. I'll describe my humiliation and tell my readers that they're reading my book because they're fat also as I was. And I'll tell them my method is simple: eat as much and lose weight while doing so.

CHAPTERS

As some argue, a linear outline isn't good a bit for many. Yes, but my take is that you can still move things around after you create it. I advise you to make a rough sketch of your idea and arrange them as you write.

But as for this, we want to create an outline that would be a good fit for a Table of Content and which would help write a sales description faster.

Your chapter should have a heading. Then you can supply the subheads after you pick a chapter heading.

A subheading is actually a section of a chapter that deals with a smaller part of the chapter's focus. You can have a chapter on writing and have three subheads focusing on writing fiction, writing nonfiction, and writing academic papers.

So, let's try to come up with chapter headings for the above weight-loss book.

Chapter one: Diagnosing the problem
Chapter two: Incorporating the solution

Chapter three: Making it consistent

It's straight from the top of my head, but let's also add subheadings to each.

Chapter one: Diagnosing the problem
- Your routine.
  - Why your day shouldn't be unplanned.
  - What you should start your day with.
  - Identifying things in your routine that won't give you time for dealing with yourself.
- Your hobbies.
  - Kinds of hobbies that'll aid gaining more weight.
  - What other hobbies you can choose that won't affect you negatively.
  - The basis of choosing a hobby that will help you lose weight.
- Your environment.
  - The environment that gives you peace.
  - The environment that enhances disaster.
  - How to know which environment you're living in.
- Your acquaintances.
  - Who do you surround yourself with?
  - Who do you live with?
  - Who do you share your shortcomings and problems with?

Chapter two: Incorporating the solution
- Your routine.
  - How to form a perfect routine.

  - o Do's and don't for your routine as a nursing mother.
- Your hobbies.
  - o How to practice your hobby without hurting your child.
  - o When you do need help while practicing your hobby.
- Your environment.
  - o How to change environments.
- Your acquaintances.
  - o What different people mean to you.
  - o How to ask people for help.
  - o When you have to demand help.

Chapter three: Making it consistent
- How to lead a consistent routinely life.
- How to not deal with people, especially your husband.
- Getting a lawsuit.
- Some thoughts on changing environments.

Now, we give it a rest. Everything was from the top of my head. If you find it a little inauthentic, bear with my weight-loss-related-topic-immuned brain. That could make a Table of Content. If you like, you can add a sentence or two to explain what you'll be dealing with while writing each chapter of your book.

CONCLUSION

"Oh, why does conclusion also matter?" I hear you ask.

Because the conclusion isn't the ending. You still need your readers to take some steps like buy your next book, subscribe to your newsletter, etc. You still need to recap all that you've told them because they've most likely forgotten. (Aside, I want to believe you don't remember all that I've said so far, can you? C'mon, can you?)

So, what goes in the outline of your conclusion?

- A recap of what you've said. Check the conclusion of this book to see what that means.
- The next step you want your readers to take.

Let's now see what we get from this book outline formula.

TITLE: The Nursing Mother's Weight Loss Formula
SUBTITLE: *Eat a lot while losing weight.*

AUTHOR'S GOAL: To enlighten nursing mothers about how they could lose weight and not gain weight, instead.

READERS: *A nursing mother who spends more time caring for her babies, but still wants to lose weight at the same time.*

URGENT PROBLEMS: Weight gain, but have less time to attend to it because of her child and other responsibility.

CONSEQUENCES: Tendency to gain more weight, if not already doing so. Feels ashamed of herself. May be subject to humiliation.

BENEFIT: Losing weight instead of gaining more. Has a beautiful image she's proud of. No humiliation.

Introduction
My story of losing 50 pounds in a week.
Humiliation as an obese.
You're reading this book because you want to lose weight.
I'll teach you to eat fat and lose weight as you do so.

Chapter one: Diagnosing the problem
- Your routine.
    - Why your day shouldn't be unplanned.
    - What you should start your day with.
    - Identifying things in your routine that won't give you time for dealing with yourself.
- Your hobbies.
    - Kinds of hobbies that'll aid gaining more weight.
    - What other hobbies you can choose that won't affect you negatively.
    - The basis of choosing a hobby that will help you lose weight.
- Your environment.
    - The environment that gives you peace.
    - The environment that enhances disaster.
    - How to know which environment you're living in.
- Your acquaintances.
    - Who do you surround yourself with?

- o Who do you live with?
- o Who do you share your shortcomings and problems with?

Chapter two: Incorporating the solution
- Your routine.
  - o How to form a perfect routine.
  - o Do's and don't for your routine as a nursing mother.
- Your hobbies.
  - o How to practice your hobby without hurting your child.
  - o When you do need help while practicing your hobby.
- Your environment.
  - o How to change environments.
- Your acquaintances.
  - o What different people mean to you.
  - o How to ask people for help.
  - o When you have to demand help.

Chapter three: Making it consistent
- How to lead a consistent routinely life.
- How to not deal with people, especially your husband.
- Getting a lawsuit.
- Some thoughts on changing environments.

Conclusion
A recap of what has been said (tell 'em what you told 'em.)

Chapter 17

Finalizing Your Outline

Now that you've filled the book outline formula, what next? You put a final touch to it. Sure, you don't have to worry about every detail, but you have to:

1. Decide What Goes in the Table of Contents

As you saw in Chapter 16, we outlined everything in a typical weight loss book. But not everything should be in the front matter. Certain things may give away the secret buried deep in the pages of your book. So what shouldn't be in the front matter of your book?

- Extreme details. An outline meant for a Table of Content shouldn't contain a thread structure of your book. That way, anyone will take one look at the Table of Contents and know everything you talked about there.

- Phrases that give away the shebang. For example, you don't want to have something like, "Why Buzz and Content are two crucial elements of an idea." When people look at it, they know what you want to talk about already and may not care for the why.

2. Add a Blurb to Each Chapter (at least)

It isn't uncommon to sample a book and find the Table of Contents vague. You should have a clear list, but don't give everything away.

You can add blurbs to it the way Rayne Hall did in *Writing Fighting Scenes.*

CHAPTER 11: UNARMED COMBAT (HAND-TO-HAND FIGHTING)
CHAPTER 12: SELF-DEFENCE
CHAPTER 13: STRENGTH, SKILL AND STRATEGY
CHAPTER 14: PSYCHOLOGICAL BARRIERS
CHAPTER 15: FEMALE FIGHTERS
CHAPTER 16: MALE FIGHTERS
CHAPTER 17: ANIMALS AND WERES
CHAPTER 18: MAKE THE READER CARE
CHAPTER 19: THE INSIDE EXPERIENCE
CHAPTER 20: ARMOUR
CHAPTER 21: FIGHT SITUATIONS
CHAPTER 22: GROUP VS GROUP, ONE VS

12. Self-Defence

Why readers love self-defence scenes. Self-defence for the skilled martial artists. Self-defence ideas the inexperienced fighter. Blunders to avoid.

13. Strength, Skill and Strategy

How much strength, skill and strategy do fighters need, and where do they get them? Blunders to avoid.

14. Psychological Barriers

Reluctance to fight. Reality shock for martial artists.' The 'freeze'.

15. Female Fighters

Reader expectations. Physical and psychological differences. Skills and backstory. Inexperienced female fighters. Different fighting

3. Add the Front and Back Matter if not Already Present

Especially for books on Amazon. You want to keep the front and back matter updated so that you have links and excerpts in the place you want it to be.

Of course, this is just meant to be an outline, but it matters. For example, the order in which you present your back matter shows the level of importance you put into it. Are you asking for reviews first? It shows you value review the most. Are you showing a link to your newsletter after the concluding paragraph of your book? It means you want more subscribers. So, you can consult your most important goal and put that first in your outline.

4. Change Some Words

Yes, this can also be an avenue for changing chapter titles or replacing a word. Imagine if I titled this chapter "What Next?" What does that mean? It doesn't show what's in it for your readers. It doesn't clearly say what they are to expect.

Compare it with "Finalizing Your Outline." You know without any doubt that this chapter will be talking about putting a final touch to your outline.

Summary

This step is suitable only after you've written your book. If you focus on this before writing a word, you may find that you end up not writing anything.

Briefly, you should plan, research, and have a rough outline to get you going in a day, and get on to writing your book. No information you've gathered about your competition will be useful if you don't write your book.

That said, after you've drawn an outline, you should proof that it's what you want.

PART 6

WRITING YOUR BOOK

Chapter 18

Writing and Editing Tips

For Heaven's sake, what are writing tips doing in an outlining book?

Because I don't want you to complain about what you have to do at the prewriting stage that you don't get anything done. This is the core message of this book:

> *Validate your idea. Plan your work. Research what you don't know about it and what you're not sure of. Create a rough outline to get you going. All in a day. Then begin writing. As you do so, the*

need to research will arise as deem fit and the outline will also evolve with it.

So, it's important that you learn to work creating an outline for your book into your writing process. Without further ado, here are the tips for you.

WRITING TIPS

1. Find your voice (and bring it to the table).

When you talk to people face-to-face, you do so with a distinct voice. People recognize it all the time. But in writing?

I'm afraid that's a mere fantasy. Writers use the same alphabet, the same dictionary of words, and of course, we speak the same language. Unlike speaking literally to someone, you can't jump on the page of your book and start screaming, "Hey, this is Alice in Wonderland, do you copy?"

And that's why it's much harder to write in a unique voice. But enough of the jabber about the importance of voice. How do you find your writing voice?

Unlike tidbits you'll find on blogs and in articles, the process of finding your writing voice is actually simple:

1. Write a lot.
2. Read a lot.

All other tips you get on finding your voice still boils down to it. So let's take 'em one by one.

1. **Write a lot.** Practice makes perfect, we all know. It's not different in writing. In fact, look nowhere else if you're looking for a perfect example of the wise saying.

   When you invite a writer who's been practicing this craft for long and another who's just getting started, you get a whooping difference in their writing. The experienced fellow didn't just grow a writing wing; he's been practicing.

   Out there, they tell us to challenge ourselves, write as if we're someone else, all that. But it's still writing. If you don't write, every tip you sink into your brain will be useless.

   Here are ways you could find your voice while writing:

   - Write in someone else's voice.
   - Copy out a popular author's work by hand.
   - Write in a different genre.
   - Write in a different point of view.
   - Write in a different emotion. (Maybe you don't get angry often and you've never brought your anger to your writing desk. Why not imagine that someone offended you and ran away. And that you're writing a letter, giving that fellow an ultimatum! Way to go, baby.)
   - Use writing prompts.

It depends on you. You could try other techniques, but if it doesn't help you write, then you can conclude that it will never help as much as writing.

2. **Read a lot.** Okay, time to let the cat out of the bag. I'm a non-native English speaker. Although we learned English in school, I laugh at the way some teachers construct their sentences back then.

   To worsen the matter, here's an excerpt from an article I wrote for an online article marketplace:

   > Without your domain and effort,you should forget about
   > your online business. You think affliate marketing don't need a blog or website but spamming? Hell no! Stop disturbing fun searchers on the web with your stupid spam messages. Have a look at why you should have a domain and invest effort before you can boast of a business. Your domain is mainly yours with
   > full access -you paid for it. Operating on a free hosting and domain,build your so-called business for a while and disappears without you even earning a penny.

I hope you don't think my writing still stink like that. So, how did I free myself from that league?

Simple: I read a lot of English writing. Oh, scratch that. **I read a lot of good English writings.** And you can testify that it's dramatically transformed my writing.

That time, I'd cuddle up somewhere with my cell phone, reading and reading. Little did I know it will pay off. I wrote that article in 2014, two years ago as at this time of writing. But I'd been reading articles online since 2011. Imagine how *suckitudinous* my writings would have been then.

Now, my point is (and I do have one), a beginning writer two years ago found his writing voice. How fast! Read blogs written by Indians, if you don't understand what I'm talking about.

Reading a lot of good books helps you:

- Write better English.
- Find your voice.

You have to believe this because I'm a living example. I'm still a non-native speaker. It may still show in my writings. But I won't carry the same stigma as an abject beginner.
And so will you, if you read good books.

2. Know your book's purpose.

Maybe you don't have to worry about this and just write with your audience in mind. I disagree. That's the point of all the research you've done on your readers. You need to know what you're giving them.

For example, I know that many writers still don't outline their work before writing, but I have to tell the abject planners that outlining aggressively isn't everything. I have to ring it every time that an outline's purpose is to aid you in writing your book.

Because I knew that purpose, I didn't appear as a better-than-thou book writer, but at the same time, I have to take a stand.

If you know your book's purpose, you'll know the kind of emotion you want to cultivate in your readers. For example, there's a way you write something meant to prick your readers' heart and make them feel guilty, and there's a way you write that same piece if you want to make them feel that they're not the only one making the same mistake.

Always remember that while writing your book.

3. Talk to your readers.

Just the way I'm talking to you now. Well, I dare say you can find your writing voice by doing that. Because it involves writing.

4. You don't have to start from the beginning.

This one took me some time to follow. Because I like starting from the beginning. It's hard, and some chapters have to be written last, no matter how you plan.

For example, I haven't written the introduction of this book. That's because the book isn't done yet. I have to get the raw draft finished before I can now sit back, look at the manuscript, and write a befitting introduction.

You may have some setback if you write in a linear mode, like:

- Being stuck where you don't know where to go next.
- Being stuck where you need a little research.
- Not having a corresponding beginning with the rest of the book.

But an outline guides your every step. You can look at your outline and decide to start from the middle, or anywhere, and you'd be fine. You don't have to start from chapter one.

5. Be in flow.

Writers are a funny bunch of people. You can't be around one for a week without noticing. Hell, even for 3 days. Why? They'll certainly write something. The urge to write will manifest and they'll start feeling guilty if they haven't written anything for a week.

I'm not talking about feeling guilty or writing every day, but about the impact that has on the writing flow.

Have you ever noticed how words seem to be magically appearing on the page some days while others it's just crickets? Go figure. It's may be because you've broken the chain of consistent writing.

What you define as writing consistently depends on you. I find that if I don't write for two days in a row, it's harder to get back to the keyboard than just missing writing for a day. I get along well even when I miss writing for a day, but not two days in a row.

For you, it may be shorter or even longer. But you should be in flow everytime so that starting your writing sessions won't be a hell of a job.

6. Stories build a bond. Be vulnerable.

I *absolutely, totally, definitely* get it if you don't want to wash your dirty linen in public. But do you what that means? That you're a robot.

How can you, a human, be error-free? Impossible. Only robots do what they're programmed to do with the greatest commitment you can imagine. And yet, robots do fail.

So, you don't have any excuse to *not* be vulnerable to your readers. It doesn't show that you're naïve or incapable of teaching them something; you're telling them about stories about how you failed **but learned from it.**

Can't think of a story to tell your readers? Here are some to help:

1. Stories about how you failed at what you're teaching them. And how you learned from it.

2. Stories about how you came about writing
that book you're working on.

3. Or pointless stories. Do you know that stories
don't have to matter to the topic at hand to be
a good one in writing? You can rant about
how hectic your day was, how angry you were
at the cabbie, and how you were just thinking
of jumping off from the 10th floor of a building.
So far that it bonds you to your audience, it's
good to go.

For more information on pointless stories,
check out this excellent article by Jon Morrow:
https://smartblogger.com/pointless-stories/

EDITING TIPS

Here we are. For now, I just want us to assume that
you've finished your book (it's a good fantasy to have,
but in reality you don't want to have it. You want to write
it.) Where should you go? What should you do? There
has to be something you can do about the manuscript
crying for help on your hard drive or your drawer, isn't
there?

1. Let it rest.

No matter how hard the manuscript cried out to you
or how real the urge to edit it at a go was, you have to
leave your manuscript in a temporary grave. It helps
your brain evict the familiarity you have with it. Although
it will surface when you get back to editing it, it won't

cause you much disaster as when you edit immediately after writing.

The longer you let it rest, the better. But the earlier you come back to it, the faster you'll get it published. So, balance leaving your work and rushing back to it. If you have the time, you can take a vacation from it for a few weeks. But if you can't, a few days won't probably hurt.

If you plan on taking a few days off, you shouldn't write anything then. Because too much of information clogging your brain wouldn't help you when you come back to edit. Unless you want to hire a professional editor, which you should consider doing.

2. Change location and medium.

When you begin editing, if you're using the same medium, maybe a computer, you'll wonder how no days you've taken are helping you now. You'll find your brain skipping words, sentences, and even paragraphs. Because it's accustomed to it.

Changing location prior to editing and using another medium will help with that. If you've written your work on a computer, print it out and start editing with a pen (not pencil! and no eraser, okay?)

If you've written it by hand, you can hire a fast typist on Fiverr and edit on your computer.

3. Following the Editing Sequence.

What's editing about? Fixing typos and replacing weaker words? Not.

The sequence to editing your work is:

1. **Developmental editing.** This is editing your work based on the overall picture. Does it go in line with the purpose? Did you get across everything you should? Can readers do what you've written in all of those pages after reading your book?

   Developmental editing is the most expensive editing of all because it's the hardest to fix. Others? You can grab a checklist or template or something to work things out. But developmental editing? No, there's no checklist for your work, except you actually do a developmental edit.

   Here are what you could focus on while doing a developmental editing for your book:

   - Is there a way you could have rearranged something in your book? Maybe it's even the entire chapters.

   - Is your book's content consistent? Do they validate themselves?

   - Did you clearly state your ideas and do they flow easily into the next one?

   - Did you stick to an English dialect throughout the book? Or you use a UK spelling here and over there, it's a phrase in US English? This is where you'll check that.

- Is your tone clear? Did you stick to the conversational type of writing?

- Did you often repeat ideas? Why?

2. **Line editing.** This is where you'll carefully edit your work so that it flows and is tight.

   Line editing focuses on removing verbosity in your writing, rewording paragraph, and making the book's content easy-to-read.

   For an example of line editing, check out this article: https://smartblogger.com/editing-tips/

3. **Copyediting.** This is where you agonize over every word. You'll check the authenticity of a word over the other. You'll insert all links. You'll verify all claims. Copyediting makes the content even tighter because it takes each sentence and slices it into many parts without losing clarity.

   In line editing, you may have taken a paragraph or two and replaced it with a sentence. In copyediting, you shorten, tighten, and make every sentence clearer.

4. **Proofreading.** This is where you'll proof that your book doesn't have grammatical errors or typo. Most of the errors would have been dealt with during the previous stage of editing, but it's now time to find the little annoying

member that haunts your readers while reading your work.

Sometimes, copyediting, line editing, and proofreading are rolled into one stage of editing and done at the same time. But at least, you should edit your manuscript twice.

4. Join a writing or critique group.

If you can't afford to hire a professional editor right now, you can find some group to join where you can receive feedback on your writing.

Usually, the other authors in the group serve as beta readers to other authors. If you ask me, beta readers are good if you want developmental editing. They're just reading your work and maybe they don't have the same experience as you have. They'll point out how vague your explanations were and/or what you could do to fix that.

As for the other editing, it takes curious eyes and determined mind to find a perfect match for you.

It won't hurt if you learn how to do it yourself at first. For that, I recommend *Copyediting for Indie Authors: A How-to Guide of Ten Top Tips to Save Time and Money and Make Your Book Look Professionally Copyedited* by Messenger, Jack and Lee Messenger, Brigitte.

That book talks more than copyediting a book. You can also use it as a checklist for line editing your book.

5. Read your work aloud.

I know it sounds awkward, ridiculous, and weird. But it works. The reason is that you catch errors you wouldn't catch with your eyes by reading your work aloud.

You'll discover sentences that don't flow, words that are out of place, and grammatical errors.

I advise you to find a quiet and solitary place to read your manuscript aloud. You won't probably notice developmental ho-hums, but copy and line editing are a sure thing.

If you can't read your work aloud, then…

6. Use NaturalReader for reading aloud and Grammarly for correcting typos.

NaturalReader is a software that reads aloud any text you put into it in an almost natural way. The premium version has the ability to convert your manuscript to an mp3 file so that you can listen to it at your leisure and without opening NaturalReader. You can check it out here:
http://www.naturalreaders.com/download.html

Grammarly, on the other hand, helps you fix typos on the page. It has a native app, an MS Word add-on, and a plugin compatible with Firefox, Chrome, etc. If you install the native app, you'll have to open it to use. If you install an MS Word add-on, you need to open Word, connect to the internet, and enable it. Then it will start showing you how to fix it your errors. You can check out Grammarly here: http://grammarly.com/

7. Don't agonize, ship, and begin writing another book.

When you've done your absolute best, including getting help from others, in polishing your work to make it shine, you can ship it out and stop worrying about nothing.

At worse, a furious reader would send you an email, lamenting how your work's full of typos. You could even invite them to keep an eagle eye out for it, just the way I did in chapter one. And if you get any email notifying you of errors in your book, do fix it as soon as possible to avoid getting email on that same thing again.

Then begin writing another book, because that's our job as a writer. It doesn't matter if the one you sent out didn't sell. If you're a real writer, you'll keep writing.

So get over with obsessing with editing your book and start writing another.

PART 7
CASE STUDY

Chapter 19

From Planning to Final Outline

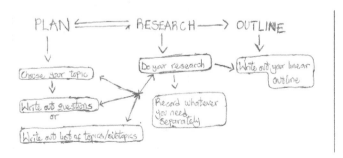

PLAN ⟵⟶ RESEARCH ⟶ OUTLINE

Choose your topic

Write out questions
or

Write out list of topics/subtopics

Do your research ⟶ Write out your linear outline

Record whatever you need separately

As I've said throughout this book, the first step of the book-writing process is conceiving an idea. After I got the idea that I wanted to write a book on planning, researching, and outlining a book, I checked on Amazon where I'll publish it and see that there are lots of outlining books, too. Some were free, while some ranged from two bucks to five bucks. And I checked their ranks and saw that it was good. I also checked the monthly searches for different keywords for my book. So, I decided I wanted to write it.

1. Planning Stage

Right there, I sketched the three topic covered in this book. You can find the sketch below:

188

As you can see, the topic was still bare. Still no introduction or the additional chapters you'll find in this book. And it's a good thing. It shows that you can expand more on a topic and write it a better way, if you approach it a better way.

After sketching, I went on to open a folder for the book. That's where everything about the book goes. First, I like to open subfolders in the parent folder. You can see the cover with label "Cover." That's where the cover issues goes, nothng else. You can also see that the folder is still parent folder is still named "Plan, Research, and Outline Your Nonfiction Book." That's a working title and I'll change it when I publish the book.

Then, I must tell you that I didn't create a timeplan for this book. Although I didn't plan it on paper, I worked toward finishing the first draft at an almost steady pace.

Can you see how planning a book seems to be simple? Simple but not easily done. Remember where I said your instinct would tell you what to plan? It holds true for me, too. I sketched the idea, organized the files in a folder, and that was all.

I didn't plan a launch team because I didn't have one. What I needed to research was the sketch itself, because I didn't want to miss anything (**cue fear of missing out.**) To me, the planning process even took some time. But it will be lesser as I write more books.

2. Researching Stage

Researching doesn't have to be tedious or time-consuming. It could last some minutes to a few hours if you use the internet—the home of millions of information, to not exaggerate.

So, I took the internet and Googled "how to plan a book." To me, when you say, "planning a book," it means you're preparing to do something. But preparing to do what? And there's the case of actually preparing something. What do you do while preparing to do something for your book?

Most aricles I read priortized outlining or making a chapter-by-chapter outline. Huh? So, that's the plan? Something wasn't connecting here. Planning is what you do before you do another thing, but making a chapter-by-chapter outline already has a name, "outlining."

I had to stand out from all that. Not necessarily prove all those people wrong. So, I created my theory that you plan your book first. I'd since known about sketching (I was a maths and technical drawing guru in high school) and I decided to use that theory in it. Artist sketch their drawing first before actually drawing it. I sketch my drawings before drawing the neat ones in technical drawing. Even in mathematics, I had to sketch how constructing an imbecillic trapezium would look like before I plot my way onto the page.

Then next is to research. Not everything at once, though. You may need to research as you write your book. But most times, you'd have covered most things you need to research.

Note that I said earlier that some topics are very controversial. What I'm writing about is a thorough example. Some people feel outlining is a waste of time while some others feel you have to write a novel-length outline before writing a book. Some feel that outlining is part of outlining while others think it's different.

You don't have to agree with nor believe in either. You have to take a stand.

My stand is that you have to plan some things. Then research. And after that, outline your book. I believe you don't have to write the perfect outline from the beginning because it will evolve as you write. I believe you don't have to research for days before you start writing. In fact, I've showed you what to do when the need to research arises while writing. Overall, I believe you can do all that's written in a day. Why? Because you can do that while writing. In fact, you're in charge of everything. You can decide to spend any time you want on any of planning, researching, or outlining your book.

I stood on that when I began writing this book.

3. Outlining Stage

The first outline I began to work with was in form of the sketch. It was a list of questions. See it here:

What is research?
What to look for while
researching?
- facts
- statistics
- answers.
How do I research?
Where do I research?
spoiler: anywhere.
How do I know that this
research is turning into an
excuse or procastination?
What do I do when the need
for research arises while
writing? answer: leave a note.

What is planning?
Spoiler: your schedule.
How do I plan my book?
What isn't planning?
What's the difference between
planning and outlining?

What is outlining?
Should I outline or not?
How do I outline my book?
The two methods of outlining
your book:
- linear way
- question way

Plan, Research, and Outline Your Nonfiction Book in a Day

At some point, I started thinking how to divide the outline into sections. I thought about how articles were structured: introduction, body, and conclusion. Then I thought I had to have something like that for my outline. Only that I'll remove the conclusion and retain introduction and body.

Then I had to determine what would go into the introduction and body. General questions and issues are generally an introduction to the body of an article. So, I decided that the introduction part will include general issues and questions, and the "body" part will include how to do it, for example, "how to research."

I decided to first call the introductory part, for example, "Overview of Planning Your Book," and the body, for example, "How to Plan Your Book."

Remember I talked about the decision of adding some topics to this book? They were:

- From vague idea to validated idea.
- Writing tips.
- Editing tips.

That was that version. The outline took another turn when I added more things and reworded some chapter titles.

Some of the things I added are:

- Your Why.
- The #1 Habit That Makes All The Difference.
- The Friction of Starting; The Lack of Friction of Stopping.
- The #2 Elements of A Bestselling Idea
- How to Create A Compelling Title.

Adekunle

- Writing and Editing Tips.
- From Planning to Final Outline: How I Planned, Researched, and Outlined This Book.

I also divided the outline into parts:

- Part 1: Introduction.
- Part 2: Pre-planing Stage.
- Part 3: Planning Your Book.
- Part 4: Researching Your Book.
- Part 5: Outlining Your Book.
- Part 6: Writing Your Book.
- Part 7: Case Study.
- Part 8: Conclusion.

Dividing the outline in parts isn't rocket science. If you look at it closely, you'll notice that it's almost every step of the book-writing process and including Case Study.

Summary

I think you've gained something from the example I've laid above and gained something. Your book-writing process shouldn't be complicated. It should be simple and easier with each book you write.

You shouldn't obsess on anything because perfectionism is your enemy.

Chapter 20

Summary of Action Steps

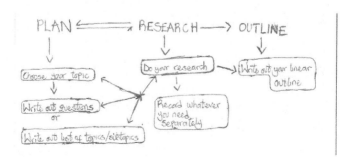

Nothing's better than having a resource list of what to do and when to do it. I created this chapter for that purpose. It's meant to be a reference list of the step-by-step actions in this book.

Not every other part is summarized here, but the ones you need to take action only. A timeline's beside each step but I want to tell you that it doesn't have to take that long.

Even as I was being realistic in sharing the time appropriately, it wasn't up to 12 hours. Because it doesn't have to take that long. If you know what you're doing, you should be able to do what would enable you to start writing immediately in 5 hours.

Most of what you're supposed to do should be after or while writing. If you do them before writing, you're shooting yourself in the foot. And that's what most people think they have to do.

Unless you're writing a book based on case studies, research doesn't have to take more than 5 hours before you begin writing. If we're being realistic.

So, all the timeframe written here are somehow realistic in nature. Let's get started.

#1: Pre-Planning Stage

This is where you'll…

*1: Find and validate your idea. (Two hours.)

Writing starts with first getting ideas that you can turn into books and confirming that it has a chance of

selling. If you keep a journal of ideas, you can skip the
"find" part. You'll have already had ideas.

*2: Brainstorm a working title (before writing—30 minutes) and compelling title (after writing.)

The idea of coming up with the perfect title before
writing a word seem stupid to me. You don't know what
angle your book might take. You don't even know how
the mini-topics you've outlined would turn out.

So, you're better advised to go with any title and
start writing.

#2: Planning Stage

Planning here, as talked about earlier, can be
anything from securing your files together, to preparing
for launch, to planning your writing sessions.

*1: Organize your files. (5-10 minutes.)

Organizing your files simply means putting your
book documents in a single folder, whether virtual or
physical. For your virtual files, create a folder where you
can easily find and you can create subfolders as I do to
deepen the level of organization you have for your book.
For example, I have a folder for cover files inside the
book's main folder.

If you're using physical files, bind them together.
Everything. From your research paper, to cover samples
you swiped for it, to outlines. Keep everything together.

This shouldn't take you more than 10 minutes. Remember that you can still reorganize later.

*2: Organize a launch team.

This doesn't have a timeline because you continue to do it even after launch. You continue to do it book launch after book launch. If you don't have one, don't stress over that before writing your book. In fact, it's better to write a book that people want and build a launch team after writing it. By that, you'll know what promise to make, so won't overpromise.

*3: Sketch your idea. (One hour.)

Again, after you've found a feasible idea, it's time to sketch it. A sketch is used by painters, artists, and architects to prepare for the real work. If they can sketch in preparation for doing the real work, I recommend you to do the same.

In the planning stage, sketching an idea means doing a brain dump of everything you know about an idea. You'll see the skeleton of your idea and know what part you don't know or aren't sure of. Then...

*4: Draw a research to-do list. (30 minutes.)

You can't write a whole book without doing a single research, even if it's just a mere fact checking. If you discover that you don't know anything about a part of your sketch, include it in your research to-do list. It will help you when you begin to do the research.

*5: Plan your time. (One hour.)

Not everybody plans each writing session because
some writers loathe planning and would rather opt for
pantsing. That's great if you know how to use it well, but
I doubt you wouldn't need to plan your time.

You don't necessarily have to plan each session.
You can plan a daily word count and adhere to it.

#3: Researching Stage (Five hours.)

Research, as depicted in this book, is not what you
just do and forget. The need to research arises as you
write and you can then do it. In the researching stage,
you should…

*1: Research more about your readers.

Humans are your readers. You need to know them
as if from birth, their struggles, their dreams, and their
most urgent problem. It would enable you to solve their
problems in a unique way as well as write a sales letter
that sells faster.

*2: Research more about your competitors.

To stand out among your competitors, you have to
know what they are doing and do something different. A
market needs competition. So, no matter how many
people go into it, you can still command attention, but in
a lesser way. In case there's no other competitive book
out there, it's a sign that the market is not viable.

*3: Research the facts.

You know the research to-do list you drew in the planning stage? Yes, go research about everything on that list now. You may spend some time tinkering around, but that shouldn't stop you from beginning to write.

To me, you should focus on a chapter or section, research it, and start writing. That way, research won't be a barrier to your writing.

#4: Outlining Stage (Two hours.)

Outlining is important to getting the job done: writing your book from start to finish. But you don't have to worry about it. Your first outline would likely be thrown in the trash. And the second, third, fourth. Because it will evolve as you write, okay? So, you should…

*1: Choose an outlining tool.

Your word processor is a lousy outlining tool. Even a spreadsheet won't get the job done. Hence, the reason to choose a tool. This shouldn't take you more than five minutes. Plus the downloading and installation time, it shouldn't take more than 30 minutes of your time.

*2: Create a rough outline so that you can begin writing ASAP.

That's the beauty of being able to tweak your outline anytime you want. If you agonize over every aspect of your outline and work your ass on getting it right the first time, you're shooting yourself in the foot. You should draw a rough outline and start writing. If you get to a stage where the outline doesn't help you go from here to there, sit back and tweak it. Add more details. Write a short blurb. But write consistently.

*3: Arrange items as you go.

Arrange items as you write your book. You could move things around. You could delete sections. You could add more items as you wish. Most importantly, you could rearrange items in the order you want.

*4: Use the book outline formula.

You should be nearing the end of your book before planning to do this. Why? It sidetracks you. Instead of writing, you're plotting. It's important, but writing is what makes all the difference. Sure, you plot and plan and outline in fiction, but you can minimize it in nonfiction. For example, you could make a list and still be able to write a nonfiction book with it. But in fiction, a list won't help much.

With the book outline formula, you can write your Table of Contents using it, and that's why you should wait after you finish writing your book. If you do it while still writing your book, possibly you'll still tweak it. Or abandon it.

*5: Add some final touches.

Even after you think your outline, which you want to use for your Table of Contents, is perfect, you can to do more make it better. You'll proof, replace words, rephrase, etc.

Summary

To recap again, in simple steps, this is how to plan, research and outline your nonfiction book in a day.

#1: Pre-planning stage.

- Find and validate your idea.
- Brainstorm a working title.

#2: Planning stage.

- Organize your files.
- Organize your launch team.
- Sketch your idea.
- Draw a research to-do list.
- Plan your time.

#3: Researching stage.

- Research about your readers.
- Research about your competitors.
- Research facts.

Plan, Research, and Outline Your Nonfiction Book in a Day

#4: Outlining stage.

- Choose an outlining tool.
- Create a rough outline.
- Arrange items as you write.
- Use the book outline formula.
- Add some final touches.

And voila! You have an outline to get you going in a day. I urge you to check and download the free worksheet at the back of this book so that you can work efficiently with this book.

PART 8

CONCLUSION

Chapter 21

Tying Everything Into A Glorious Knot

I believe you've learned something from this book. Thank you for giving me time out your time to read this book. And I hope my technique helps you write that book faster.

To make writing your book even faster, I have specially made...

The Worksheet

I've made a worksheet for you so that your work will be faster. The worksheet takes you through what I've talked about in this book and you can print it for personal use.

You can download it here: http://bit.ly/1WEAeAa
I want to remind you.

Perfectionism is your enemy; don't ever allow it. Don't feel obliged to get everything perfect at first. As I said, things will shape up when you're writing your book.

To recap all what I've said in this book, here are the main highlights:

Part 1: Introduction

- You should make **honing your skills** your number one reason and purpose for writing a book. All others come second.

- If you don't write, nothing changes. **Writing makes the difference** between making money, acquiring customers, and becoming a bestselling author.

- Just **open the damn document**, boy! And get going. One word. Two. A paragraph. A section. Before you know it, you now have a chapter. You avoid the friction of starting that way.

- If you discover that you can't stop the flow, **tell 'em what you told 'em.**

Part 2: Pre-planning Stage

- The two elements of a bestselling idea are: content and buzz. Go figure!

- You create a compelling title with a combination of clarity and discoverability. Go figure!

Part 3: Planning Your Book

- Planning isn't outlining, researching, and organizing your files, to name a few.

- You plan your book by organizing your files, organizing a launch team, sketching your idea, determining what you need to research, creating a timeplan, and creating an on-the-go kit.

Part 4: Researching Your Book

- You can't do without researching, no matter how small.

- You research more than facts. You research about your readers, competitions, and facts.

- You research on internet, in libraries, by interviewing, and by reading periodicals and dailies.

Part 5: Outlining Your Book

- Outlining is a lifesaver for a writer while it totally spoils the fun for another writer.

- There are probably thousands of outlining tools out there, but you just have to choose one and you're set.

- Arrange your outline in a senseible order.

- Use the book outline formula for maximum effect.

- Outlines also need proofs, okay?

Part 6: Writing Your Book

- If I can give just a tip here, it'll be writing in writing mode (using the left brain) and editing in editing mode (using the right brain.) Try to do the two together and you've plotted your sabotage.

Part 7: Case Study

- What can I say? I followed what's in this book.

Free Worksheet

To download the Plan, Research, and Outline Worksheet, go here: http://bit.ly/1WEAeAa

Did You Like This Book?

Let everyone know by posting a review on Amazon. Just open the link below and it will take you directly to the reviews page where you'll write your review. It'll take less than five minutes:

http://amzn.to/1TUMF7w

Other Books by the Author

I have written a few books in the Young Writers' Craft Guides series. You can see them by opening this link in your browser: **http://bit.ly/1Ou19fw**

How to Write A Short Story.

Do you struggle to write your story? Do you lose track of whatever to say whenever you sit down to write your story? Here's a guide to your rescue.

It doesn't even want to believe you know how to write a story or what a story is. In an easy-to-read manner, the information distilled in this book will take you from finding ideas for your story to plotting to writing it.

No doubt that you could wake up one day, pick up your pen and notepad, and start scribbling away. No problem if you're writing exclusively for for yourself. But there could be a problem if you'll be sharing your story with the world.

What if you could learn how to write a story from scratch? What if you could build in-depth characters, settings and conflicts that catch readers' mind and build their suspense? What if you could avoid writing fiction jargon altogether, even while writing exclusively for yourself?

Avoid the most dangerous itch, which originates from your story. You can sell a crappy book with some workaround for the short run, but it would backfire in the long run.

Here are some of the things you'll learn in this book:

- The essential elements of fiction
- The only way stories are conceived stories are conceived.

- How to develop three-dimensional, in-depth characters so they feel real to your readers.
- Character questionnaire to help you with you character building.
- How to create suspense-building conflicts in your story.
- What settings are and how to get setting ideas for your story.
- What a plot is, types of plots, and how to plot your story.
- How to write in different point of views.

...and more.

Excerpt from the book

CHAPTER ONE: ESSENTIALS OF FICTION

INTRODUCTION

LIKE HUMANS NEED oxygen, there are some vital elements a story (which is here, referred to as fiction) needs. It is simply: character, conflict, and setting. In a story, something has to happen to someone, somewhere, sometimes.

For easy understanding, these essentials of fiction are like the blades of a ceiling fan. They are equidistant from each other. You start with one, you're bound to meet the other two, if you want your work to be a story. Again, you can start with an idea of one; definitely, you'll get the other two in no time.

How Stories Are Conceived

As said earlier, stories are born out of a writer's imagination choices. The production of a story begins with any of the three elements mentioned.

For example, a writer may start with a character idea. A lost boy in an uninhabited jungle. Then, the ideas for conflict and settings starts setting in. What made the boy lost? Where was the jungle located? Was there a telephone at that time? What time of the day did he get lost? Would he be found before the dark? Or would he use another day lurking around there, hungry and naked?

Now, answers are different. It depends on the writer. A writer may situate the jungle in Austin, Texas, New York. Another may situate it in Australia. While another may situate it in Congo.

For example, a writer's choice might go like this: A lost boy in an uninhabited jungle in Austin.

He wandered off unknowingly from the highway when the car he and his mother were traveling in broke down. The mother has gone to find help somewhere and had left the boy there.

(If you're a smart writer with great imagination, you should have noticed another story idea popping out from that scene. **A careless mother.** If the story would be in part, that other idea might make another part.)

Another writer may start with setting ideas.

What Settings Are

Settings are the place and time a story takes place. For example, one of my stories, *Beyond Her Boundary*, took place in Ohafia Village, Abia State, Nigeria, spanning a duration of a day. The other day involved was just a headline news.

As a writer, you can start with these ideas too.

For example, your setting may be in a Friday the 13th cabin in the night. Who are/is inside the cabin? Why are they there?

A common answer may be: Julie and Hattie were inside the Friday the 13th cabin, scared. It was a night. They were hungry, but they couldn't cook inside the small cabin, or they'll die of suffocation.

From that answer, we can deduce the characters as Julie and Hattie. The time of the day was the night. The place was inside a cabin. Maybe it was even the rain outside that caused them to shiver.

The conflict they were battling was hunger and inability to cook in the small cabin. Maybe fear of the dark was even included.

Yet, another writer can start with a conflict idea.

The conflict may be a man trembling while driving home because he was going to kill his wife or send her to jail. Other questions may then come in.

Like, who was the husband? Who was the wife? Where was the home mentioned earlier? What did the wife do to deserve that furious decision? Where do they live? Where was the man driving home from?

Self-assessment 1

Begin with a character, conflict or setting idea. After conceiving, ask burning questions that will reveal the other two elements. You can use the questionnaire at the chosen element below.

Go here to buy: http://amzn.to/1R2IQbR

Generate and Validate Your Bestselling Book Idea.

From the Author

Let me just put it simply that if I'd had a kind of book like this when I was starting out, I would have been smelling bestsellers, if not had many bestsellers.

And I want to help you avoid that.

Writing a book starts with an idea: you have to have lots of it and then validate it (confirm that it would sell) before proceeding. But many authors are out there, confused as to where to find ideas they can turn into books that'll sell.

Some are plain scared (and/or lazy) to go the extra mile because either all the ideas they have aren't going to sell or that they feel they can't write a book on the ideas they keep getting.

Some are plain stuck. "So I've got this idea," they say, "where to?" Well, that's what this series will answer.

You should be able to look at the books in this series and know the next step you need to take. You should be able to read those books and know exactly what to do.

For a moment, forget about the distractions out there. You need quantity as much as you need quality, and it's all distilled here for you.

As you apply what's in this book, may you find joy in everything you write.

Excerpt from the Book

4 TIPS FOR FINDING BOOK IDEAS

If you want your book to stand a chance in the hell of iceberg of books out there, you have to focus on some core things. I believe if you can generate a unique book idea, find a tantalizing and attention-grabbing title, and write emotion-driven sales copy, you have given yourself a whole lot of chance against your competitions.

It's not the only thing, I know. But how many authors would do it?

"Do what?" you ask.

Do spend time to find ideas. Some authors are quite lazy that they couldn't even jot down ideas that pop into their brain. They think they can't forget it. They think it's crap. They it's too simplistic. Or, a whole lot of other vague reason.

It once happened to me. Why? Because I had so many ideas I didn't work on. It came to a time that I had to get rid of a whole jotter full of ideas, both fiction and nonfiction. And you know what? I think it's a terrible mistake. I still regret it.

How many authors would spend time to jot ideas? It doesn't matter whether they're in the bathroom, eating, or taking a walk in the Sahara Desert. What matters is to capture the ideas.

Ideas are like birds. If you don't capture them when they gently, willingly perch on the small branch of a short tree in your garden, they'll fearfully, quickly fly away. And maybe you caught a glance of them while moving away. But that's not enough. Nothing equates the presence of that bird.

To worsen the matters more, how many authors would validate their ideas? I mean, how many would look at the eBook market and see with their naked eyes that their ideas are needed?

You see, writing a book based on an idea that the market doesn't approve of is like going around, checking in front doors of people and proposing a literature to them when they have five kids at home giving them a hell of problem. Right then… I mean, right then, all they need is someone who'd help calm their kids. So to hell with… was it literature or something?

Alas! It could be an author's book. Specifically, it may be your book. How sad is that?

How many authors would research other books already published, and offer a different solid perspective? Or cater to another demographic entirely?

You see, Amazon Kindle has made life better. You could look inside as many books as have the "Look Inside" feature and see the quality of the book right away. It's not like the good ol' days when you had to buy the physical books yourself. Sure, you may check it out at bookstores. But how many bookstores would you want to visit everyday to gather the necessary research for your book.

You can't spend the whole eternity there.

Furthermore, how many of that book do you think that bookstore would have? Oh, don't you see other books competing for attention? Recipe books, weight loss books, make money, save money, invest money, and build financial wealth books, and a host of fiction books. Oh my.

Then it's the matter of other eBook platforms. Could you please "Look Inside" a Kobo eBook before you buy?

That is why you shouldn't rush to write that book. Yoou should sit, think, list out a range of ideas, and check the internet for validation.

I have something for you. So here we go.

1. Observe People's Problem

Okay, it sounds so ridiculous. I can feel it even as I'm writing this. But it works.

Think of these scenarios.

An introvert who curls up on his bed 24/7 without an ounce of courage to explore the outdoors, for… whatever reasons.

A beginning writer who's furiously searching the internet for how to publish an eBook with minimal expenses.

A fat housewife who's hellbent on losing weight to please her husnand.

Something is common to these people: they have a problem. The question is, can you solve that problem? If you ask me, it starts with you observing their problem, even if they don't come to you.

That introvert needs some inspirational book to lift his spirit. Or perhaps a funny story to lighten his mood.

That beginner needs information on publishing eBooks, distilled in an easy-to-read, easy-to-navigate eBook like the one he/she wants to publish.

That housewife needs techniques that work to combat her excess fat.

They all want the same thing: solution to their problems. And the first step you can take is to observe it. In other words, understand them, understand the problem, understand the emotions that rolls with it, understand anything worth understanding about them and their problem.

2. Try Solving the Problems

This is the sequel to #1. Why not try to solve those problems? You've seen the problems, experienced it, understood it.

Maybe you have an introvert brother. And let's assume, for a whole lot of sufficient and good reasons, that he's doing fine. How did he? Did you help with that? That's the answer to that introvert's problem. Personal stories with sprinkles of facts in it.

Maybe you've been a beginner, too. Once. Wait, you were a beginner at a point in time. Do you remember? That time when writing regularly was the hardest problem in the whole world. That time when you just wonder where your creative muse went to. That time when you stare at the screen, arms folded on your chest, waiting for inspiration.

Oh, what about the horror of formatting your books? Publishing them? Promotion them? Arghh! You already have a series of book ideas.

Maybe you were once fat. Or maybe you know how to lose weight fast. There. That's it.

Can I tell you the truth? It's never simpler than that. And wait, it's never more complicated than that. End of story.

3. Pick Your Area of "Inpertise"

Lest I forget, I checked my dictionary, but I couldn't find the word "Inpert."

The word originated when I was brainstorming with my mentor. The idea was that since you're not an "expert" yet, you can be an "inpert." Which means that instead of wearing the same wig with a college professor, you can come off as reporting what ordeal you went through, how you learned what you're narrating now, what worked for you, and what did not.

Simply put, an **inpert** is:

Someone who doesn't appear as a Know-It-All, but who, with a conscious state of mind, commits to learning every day and helping others learn what he's also learned.

Your area of expertise can be anything. Remember that you're learning and the tribe following you is learning as you.

Have you been studying how to write a Kindle book lately, but you don't yet have a slew of Kindle books under your belt? You can relate your experience.

Tell us why your techniques didn't work, if it didn't. Tell us why it worked, if it did. Tell us the "smartcuts" you'd have taken to learn it faster. This itself opens door to whatever you've been learning, whether a hobby or not, and that you're passionate about.

4. Jot Every Idea

Do simply go out with your pen and notepad. If you're tech savvy (why wouldn't you be?), you have your smartphone with you all the time.

The truth about ideas vanishing won't appear real, until it happens to you.

Many times, I've had to rack my brain, even to the point of physically hitting my head, telling my brain to dole out the idea I was looking for. Turns out, I was wrong. My brain wasn't the fault. In fact, I can atest that it was right then I began to recall everything I did in the twenty-four hour timeframe.

How I went to the bathrom, how I eat, all that. But not the words. Sometimes I'd remember it, sometimes not. But I'm urging you to save yourself brain-racking sessions by jotting every idea.

Have an idea of a military fiction? Jot it. What about weight loss? Jot it. How about making lots of money? Jot it. What about designing a book cover without designing skills? Jot it.

Two words: **jot it.**

It doesn't matter where you are or even how horrible the idea sounds. All of our idea sucks, but you'll discover how to know whether there's market for your book or not. Right now, jot that idea.

Go here to buy: **http://amzn.to/1R2IQbR**

About The Author

Hello, I'm Abraham Adekunle, an eighteen-year-old writer, author, and upcoming online entrepreneurs.

I believe starting from scratch shouldn't be a hit-or-miss game for young writers and authorpreneurs like me, because it has been for me. But I started writing the Young Writers' Craft Guides Series to help with that.

Accordingly, writers should be able to look at that series and know the exact step they should be taking on their way to publishing. They should be able to read the books and do what it promised after they finish it.

That is my goal and it can't survive without your support. To join my email list, go here: http://bit.ly/25rnhfR

If you'd rather email me, kindly forward any correspondence to youngwriterscraft@gmail.com

Want a PDF Version?

Would you like a PDF version of this book? Well, there's no way I can know whether you bought it or not. Except you write a review.

So, open this link: http://amzn.to/1TUMF7w and write your review, either positive or negative. Then send an email to youngwriterscraft@gmail.com

Your PDF version will be forwarded to you as soon as I confirm your review.

Questions? Comments?

Help make the next edition of this book even better. Email suggestions to youngwriterscraft@gmail.com

Made in the USA
Middletown, DE
25 March 2021